Every Day Is New

PRAYERS and REFLECTIONS for ORDINARY TIME

MICHAEL McGIRR

Paulist Press NOVALIS

For Sr Angela Slattery and Sr Jane Kelly –
– seekers of truth and doers of justice

Cover design: Audrey Wells
Cover photograph: iStock/by_adr
Interior photographs: © Michael McGirr except p. 7 (Pexels/Pixabay), p. 12 (Bluehouse Skis/Pixabay) and p. 26 (PublicDomainPictures/Pixabay)
Adaptations to the original layout: Audrey Wells

Published in Canada by Novalis

Publishing Office
1 Eglinton Avenue East, Suite 800
Toronto, Ontario, Canada
M4P 3A1

Head Office
4475 Frontenac Street
Montréal, Québec, Canada
H2H 2S2

en.novalis.ca

Cataloguing in Publication is available from Library and Archives Canada

ISBN: 978-2-89830-259-6

Printed in Canada.

Library of Congress Cataloging-in-Publication Data available upon request.

ISBN 987-0-8091-5777-8 (paperback)
ISBN 978-0-8091-8944-1 (ebook)

Published in the United States by
Paulist Press
997 Macarthur Boulevard
Mahwah, New Jersey 07430
www.paulistpress.com

We acknowledge the support of the Government of Canada.

5 4 3 2 1 29 28 27 26 25

Originally published in Australia by Garratt Publishing
32 Glenvale Crescent, Mulgrave, VIC 3170
www.garrattpublishing.com.au

Design and Typesetting by Guy Holt Design
Edited by Alex Kolasinski

ISBN 9781922484819

This book was written on the lands of the Wurundjeri people of the Kulin nation.
The author and Australian publisher pay their respects to elders past and present.

The authors and publisher gratefully acknowledge the permission granted to reproduce the copyright material in this book. Every effort has been made to trace copyright holders and to obtain their permission for the use of copyright material.

Contents

Introduction

One Life, a movie directed by James Hawes (2023), tells the true story of Nicholas Winton, the kind of figure who gives us all hope. There isn't a spark of glamour or a moment of self-promotion in his entire life. He is the kind of person you would never notice on the bus. Nevertheless, he managed to save over 690 Jewish children from Prague in the days of Nazi horror. The film shows how Winton created community, a network of tenacious people who made this possible. For all his modesty, he was not easily deterred.

At one time, Winton says, 'I am an ordinary man, and we are an army of the ordinary.'

An army of the ordinary can achieve far more than a parade of people with an inflated sense of their own importance. We are fed by the baker who turns up every day at 4 a.m. while most of us are still asleep, not by the celebrity with a carefully crafted image.

The Christian community mostly comprises ordinary people. Jesus compared the kingdom of God to yeast in bread (Matt 13:33). You never notice the yeast itself, but it makes the whole loaf rise and become lighter. It is spread throughout the mixture, not kept in one sealed-off section of it. Jesus was a poet with a gift for wonderful imagery: the seed, the pearl, the treasure, the fish and so on. Yeast is a terrific image. It makes me think of people who faithfully serve the community, year in and year out. Ordinary people can be quite extraordinary.

When we consider the Christian year, this is not quite the meaning that gives rise to the expression 'ordinary time'. Ordinary Time refers to the 33 or 34 weeks of the year that are neither Advent, Lent nor Easter time. It is not fair to think of Ordinary Time as the leftovers. After all, Ordinary Time includes over half the year and embraces all sorts of special days and feasts, including the Season of Creation in September.

In this context, the word 'ordinary' means 'in order', reflecting our belief that the orderly marking of time is one of the ways we prevent life from falling into random chaos. Every year, our Easter candle has an *alpha* and *omega* inscribed on it, the first and last letters of the Greek alphabet. They represent the first and last moments of time. In between is inscribed the current year, a mere whistlestop on the long journey from the beginning to the end of the universe. We use time to find our place, to celebrate order.

This is a natural thing to do and extends far beyond religious communities: birthdays, anniversaries and even monthly meetings are among the ways nearly everyone makes order around the world. It is also part of our living in tune with the sun, moon and stars. Seasons come and go; no sooner has one year ended than another begins. We are all creatures, and our sense of natural order helps us recognize our small part in creation. Ordinary Time is a celebration of our creatureliness.

Nevertheless, there is still something profound about the very experience of ordinariness. In one of his best-known poems, George Herbert (1593–1633) conjures up many images of prayer. One of them is 'heaven in ordinary'. Our faith begins with an ordinary young woman, in an ordinary house, in an ordinary town saying yes to the most outlandish invitation. It continues with our own daily experience of God, a subtle, elusive and beautiful presence. God sits with us, eats with us, walks with us and works with us. Every breath renews God's gift of life to us. We have a deep need for a daily stillness that allows us to recognize this, even if only for a few minutes. The singer and activist Bono writes beautifully about prayer in his 2022 memoir, *Surrender*:

> *It's an extraordinary thing the moment of surrender. To get down on your knees and ask the silence to save you, to reveal itself to you. To kneel down, to implore, to throw yourself out into space, to quietly whisper or roar your insignificance. To fall prostrate and ask to be carried. To humble yourself with your family, your bandmates, and to discover if there's a face or name to that silence.*

Prayer is soil

The poet Mia Anderson has been at different times an actor, a shepherd and a priest. She has a wonderful work called, 'Prayer Is Scrubbing'. It ends with the line 'Prayer is soil.' That gets me thinking.

Like soil, prayer is a place from which things grow. It is also a place we get dirty: when we pray, we get down on our knees, take off our gloves and put our hands deep into the earth of life and mystery. Prayer, like soil, must be protected. It can easily be blown away by the winds of busyness and preoccupation. It also takes time, as does compost. None of our experiences of life should go into landfill. Nor should they necessarily be recycled. It is better to put them all in the compost bin and allow the worms of grace to transform them into something that gives life.

There is nothing ordinary about this. But it happens in Ordinary Time.

How you might use this book

For years, I have used the same simple structure for daily prayer. It has five steps.

- Be still. Time to switch off.
- Be grateful. This day and everything in it is a gift.
- Be open. Read the Scripture slowly, listening deeply.
- Be honest. Respond from your heart.
- Be hopeful. Let your prayer travel with you as you leave.

This small book is an invitation to surrender by taking a little time on the weekdays in Ordinary Time to read the gospel of the day and take stock of where God might be at work and at play in the ordinary experience of the day. Luckily, the gospels for the weekdays in Ordinary Time are the same from year to year. You need a copy of the New Testament to go alongside this book.* Rather, this book goes alongside the New Testament.

This book is written in the belief that *every day is new*, that God might be humming a slightly different tune in your ear than yesterday or tomorrow. God fills the present with a song, a fragrance, a whisper, a touch. We are blessed if we can appreciate God's more subtle flavours. That is what prayer is for.

There are plenty of reflections available for Advent, Lent and Easter, and many of them are terrific. There are not so many available for Ordinary Time. Hence this book, which comes as much from my need to find a structure for prayer as from anywhere else.

Each week contains a simple image. Almost all of them are pictures of graffiti and street art, some of them simple and others more elaborate. They are reminders that we are part of a broader community in which everyone is trying to create an environment of meaning. Many of these works are here today and gone tomorrow. They are included as an invitation to keep looking outwards as well as inwards.

* The Scripture quotations in this book are from the New Revised Standard Version; you are welcome to use the Bible translation of your choice for the readings.

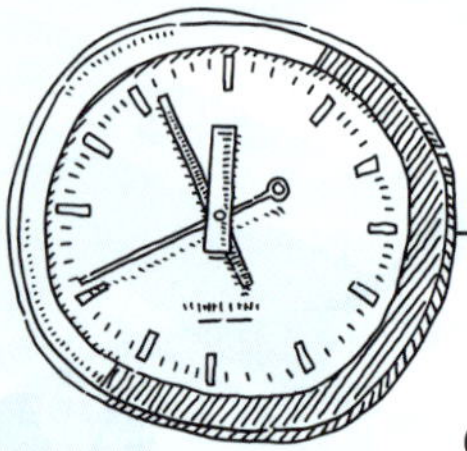

Week 1

On an ordinary day, somebody stuck a sign on the pedestrian crossing saying, 'May the LORD bless you and keep you.' Another person tried to remove it.

The words remind me that we have to choose how we will make all the crossings that lie ahead this year. We don't have to do them alone. God wants to walk closely with us.

After Christmas and the Epiphany, we pack away the tinsel and lights for another year. You know that Ordinary Time has begun when you start seeing Christmas trees left out for collection. The first credit card statement after the festivities is often a shock. We come down to earth, hopefully not with too much of a thud.

Mark's Gospel meets us in Week 1. That's a better way of putting it than saying we meet Mark's Gospel. This gospel has an uncanny ability to find us right where we are, thinking about a new year, wondering what life might hold for us in the coming days, weeks and months. We carry all the people we love into a new year. The gospel carries us.

Mark gets straight down to business. The story rolls up its sleeves right away. It has a big job to do.

Prayer for Week 1

God of my life, You have met me on the road we have journeyed together. Fill me with gratitude for the gift of another year. Keep my heart fresh and my mind hungry. Be close to me and all those I love. Amen.

May the LORD
bless you and keep
you. May

Monday
Mark 1:1–18

'The time is fulfilled ... and the kingdom of God has come near.'

It's not so easy to look in the mirror on a Monday morning and hear the words 'the time is fulfilled'. But it is. Fishermen follow a routine. The ones in today's gospel went to work on yet another predictable day; they were not expecting to hear the words 'follow me'. We are sure to hear the same words today in some way. But who will say them, and how will we respond?

Tuesday
Mark 1:21–28

'What is this? A new teaching ...'

Christians never have a Groundhog Day, let alone a groundhog year. Many things may be familiar. We may still have the same job, live in the same place, see the same people. God makes all things new, all the time. Let's keep the door of our hearts open for God's surprises, great and small.

Wednesday
Mark 1:35–39

'In the morning, while it was still very dark ...'

Jesus made time in the early morning, before the day was hot and the crowds came looking, to be alone with God. We need those times too. We need to protect them. We make appointments to see the physiotherapist and the podiatrist. We need to turn up for God as well, with all our aches and pains.

Thursday
Mark 1:40–45

'I do choose.'

The person with such a terrible skin condition was nervous. It's no wonder he lacked self-confidence; he had been excluded from community, maybe for a long time. He was lonely. But he touched Jesus' heart. We are all a bit insecure, if we care to admit it. We wonder if family and friends really love us. We carry hurts. We wonder if we, too, have a special place in God's heart. 'I do choose!' said Jesus.

Friday
Mark 2:1–12

'Jesus saw their faith ...'

Capernaum was not far from where Jesus grew up. The crowds arrived. Some of them might only have been curious about the famous local boy. The story asks us also to focus on four friends who carried a paralyzed person. It's not easy to get a stretcher onto a roof, but they persisted. The text says, 'Jesus saw their faith'. Not 'his faith'. Jesus loved these friends who would stop at nothing. If we had to choose four such people for ourselves, who would they be?

Saturday
Mark 2:13–17

'Those who are well have no need of a physician ...'

The world seems so intolerant these days. Perhaps it's a way that many of us cope with complexity, with all the raucous voices coming from every direction. It's easier to see things in black and white. It's reassuring that it was not so different in the time of Jesus. 'Why does he eat with ... sinners?' The good news is that he does eat with us. We can all be unkind, intolerant, petty and angry. We can be dishonest in relationships. We all need the doctor.

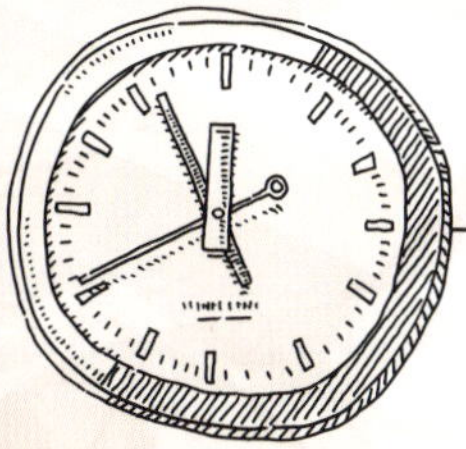

Week 2

It's only a short time since we made our new year's resolutions. Perhaps you don't take part in that kind of thing. Perhaps you've made so many resolutions over the years and haven't kept them. You have lived inside your own head and heart for a long time and now you are ready to laugh a little at your own unrealistic expectations of yourself. Maybe this year, at long last, you are ready to leave some of the decisions to God.

In a laneway behind a shopping centre, somebody has painted the words 'Good' and 'thanks'. They have taken time over it. The words are colourful and bright, cheering up the area behind the shops where there is no need for window dressing and signs with special offers. There is welcome among the weeds.

These two words could be a great resolution for the year. To see the good in the world and in people. To taste the good in every meal. To feel the good in every hug. To hear the good in what people are really trying to say, even when it comes out wrong. And, above all, to give thanks. Give thanks to the Lord, for God is good.

Mark's Gospel, our companion in these days, is an endless stream of encounters with people and places. Jesus moved around at a colossal speed. He found good everywhere. He was grateful for it.

Prayer for Week 2

God of my diary, Help me to make time for you. To order my life so that the important things come first and we spend simple time together. Amen.

Monday
Mark 2:19–22

'New wine into fresh wineskins!'

Jesus calls us to take a risk. The Pharisees, who were good people, became stuck in a narrow and inflexible way of understanding God. Jesus believed that there are times to live in the moment, to celebrate the opportunities life presents us, whether that is the new beginning of a wedding or just a glass of wine! Let us venture boldly into the arms of an adventurous God.

Tuesday
Mark 2:23–28

'Have you never read ...'

Jesus really knew Scripture. The story of David spoke to him powerfully. Jesus understood that there is much more in Scripture than rules and regulations. There are moments of breathtaking freedom and creativity. The Pharisees seemed to have forgotten that. They found Jesus threatening, as – to be honest – we sometimes do as well.

Wednesday
Mark 3:1–6

'... grieved at their hardness of heart ...'

The Sabbath is a great idea. It's more than a month since Christmas, and maybe some of us already need a bit of time off to ourselves to recharge the batteries. The wisdom of the Scriptures is terrific: life needs a rhythm, and, from the creation of the world, part of that rhythm is rest. The people Jesus met didn't seem to understand this. Surely getting angry and plotting a murder is work. It is certainly exhausting. They couldn't let go.

Thursday
Mark 3:7–12

'... all who had diseases ...'

Many of us don't like crowds, but there are plenty of ways in which we are all part of a crowd. We share more with people we don't like than we often care to admit. We are all afflicted, and to be honest, we don't mind pushing our way to get what we want. Let's imagine we get a moment with Jesus to tell him about what we truly need, deep down. What would we say?

Friday
Mark 3:13–19

'... called to him those whom he wanted ...'

The list of names of Jesus' closest friends is wonderful. It reminds us that nobody is just a number in the kingdom of God. There is no recorded message saying 'your call is important to us' while we wait for 45 minutes to speak to a person. There is no ChatGPT to tell our story or to write our prayers. It is all personal. Jesus loved friendship. He also expected his friends to make a difference. The same applies to us this very day.

Saturday
Mark 3:20–21

'... people were saying, "He has gone out of his mind."'

It helps to know that even Jesus had problems with his relatives. If we haven't argued with a relation, or been misunderstood or frustrated by one, then we don't really know the meaning of the word 'family'. Family is both one of God's greatest blessings and one of God's most serious challenges. Yet, Scripture tells us that Jesus went home. His father, Joseph, probably made the kitchen table. It must have heard many stories.

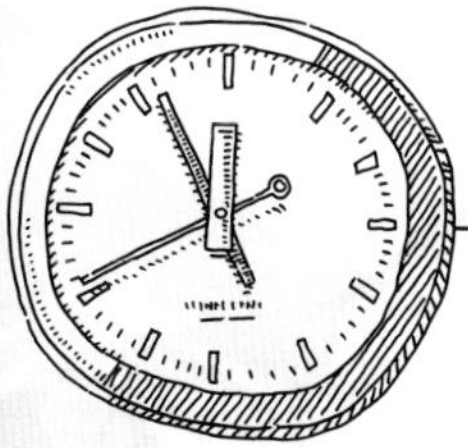

Week 3

Mary MacKillop was Australia's first saint. She could well be the patron of Ordinary Time, a person who opened many little schools in small, isolated communities. A woman who created safe spaces for women and children fleeing domestic violence. A woman who built community, even with difficult people. A person who knew that the basics of life were not available to everyone.

Right opposite the place where Mary MacKillop was born in Melbourne in 1842, somebody has posted a sign that says, 'Please be awesome'. It's a welcome relief from somebody telling us 'I am awesome'. It's also an invitation: to truly be oneself is to inspire awe in others.

The people in Mark's Gospel are constantly awestruck:

'Who is this?'

'We have never seen anything like this.'

'And everyone was amazed.'

'They were utterly and completely dumbfounded …'

'He did not know what to say …'

The gospel asks us each to be awesome in our own way. Mark concludes his gospel by saying that we will handle snakes and drink poison without harm. These days, we might say we will stand up to bullies, work with people we find difficult and never give up hope. Mark ends with a hint of the adventures to come: 'the Lord working with them.'

Prayer for Week 3

God of my days, Draw me deeper into the mystery of your love. Be with me in times of fear and doubt. Show me the path to life. Free me from the worries that don't help anyone. Amen.

PLEASE
BE
AWESOME
FETTBURGER.COM
FETTBURGER.COM
FETTBURGER.COM

Monday
Mark 3:22–30

'If a house is divided against itself ...'

The human family is so deeply divided that life can feel more painful than it should. There is a new word doing the rounds: *angertainment*. It refers to media and other groups that exploit anger as a way of hooking in business. Anger is a highly addictive drug. Jesus seemed to have realized this. What can we do today to help the world detox?

Tuesday
Mark 3:31–35

'Here are my mother and my brothers!''

Perhaps Jesus wasn't really having a dig at his own family. They were clearly worried about him. He was, as we say these days, 'out there'. He was simply saying that he was open to a close and heartfelt relationship with anyone who shared his passion to put God at the centre of their life. God's will wouldn't be easy for them. It would require a deep surrender, as it does for us all.

Wednesday
Mark 4:1–20

'Other seed fell into good soil ...'

It takes time to produce rich soil. Anyone with a compost bin knows that. You need a lot of grass clippings and leftovers; you also need to let the worms work at their own pace. What does it mean to become the rich soil that will nurture God's life within us? This parable tells us. Not to be too rocky. Not to be shallow. Not to be too anxious or worried about material things. To be as warm as the fertile earth. It takes years of practice. Be patient.

Thursday
Mark 4:21–25

'...not on the lampstand?'

There is an old saying that we are only as sick as our secrets. There are parts of our lives of which we are not proud. We'd be embarrassed if people knew about them. Jesus asks us to be honest with God. After all, there's no point lying to God. Putting a lamp under a bed or tub is dangerous – especially a bed. They could catch fire. Jesus wants us to be a light to the world and to ourselves.

Friday
Mark 4:26–34

'With what can we compare the kingdom of God?'

I had no idea what a mustard seed looked like until I discovered Dijon mustard, and sure enough, they are tiny. That's what makes a mustard seed a great image of the kingdom of God. From the smallest gestures of kindness, the most subtle colour of nature, the nervous start of a campaign for justice, an email to a person with whom we have had a misunderstanding, the kingdom of God grows and grows. It is growing today, at the end of the week. It does not wait for the weekend.

Saturday
Mark 4:35–41

'Why are you afraid?'

Jesus' friends asked him if he really cared about them. He replied by asking them why they were worrying. So many relationships are like this. Someone is tired and grumpy, and we wonder if they like us. Someone else forgets our date to meet for coffee, and we think they are treating us badly. Another person hasn't returned the book we loaned to them. Jesus often told people not to be so anxious. We should take those words to heart.

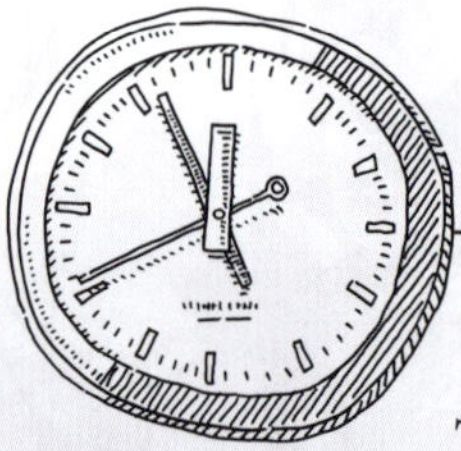

Week 4

This week we are going to meet an extraordinary gathering of people: the man called Legion, a synagogue official called Jairus, a woman with a hemorrhage, Peter, James, John, narrow-minded people from Jesus' hometown, Herod, Herodias and John the Baptist – the crowd that follows Jesus. They represent many points on a compass. What could they all possibly have in common?

Let's think for a few minutes about the people we are likely to come across in our own lives this week. The people we live with, the neighbours, perhaps the barista who makes our morning coffee, work colleagues, perhaps a doctor or pharmacist, friends. We could add to that the people with whom we simply share our world: people in the supermarket, other passengers on the bus, an Uber driver. Again, what do we all share?

The characters in Mark's Gospel all share a deep hunger and longing for connection or community. Some, such as Herod, are blind. Others, such as John the Baptist, are wide-eyed. Still others are in the process of opening their eyes. The same probably applies to our own encounters. In every case, a need for love and belonging allows God an opportunity to get close to us. Let us pray that our honesty will allow God that opportunity this week.

Prayer for Week 4

God of my fears, Work within me to create in my heart the deep soil in which your love will grow and become a source of life and light for both friends and strangers. Amen.

Monday
Mark 5:1–20

'Go home to your friends ...'

It is interesting how often the gospels mention clothes. They tell a story about the person who wears them. When we encounter Legion, a man with acute mental health issues, he is naked. He lives among the dead. At the end, he is fully clothed and 'in his right mind'. This is a story about his journey from loneliness to community. How do we make that journey ourselves?

Tuesday
Mark 5:21–43

'... be healed of your disease.'

The woman with a hemorrhage has been exploited by doctors, all of them men. She has used all her money and experienced nothing but pain, yet she continues to hope. Jesus asked for nothing from her. He only wanted her freedom. Jesus wants the same for us. He wants to lead us out of unhealthy and manipulative relationships.

Wednesday
Mark 6:1–6

'He was amazed at their unbelief.'

Jesus was surprised by his reception in his hometown. People expected him to be just like his brothers and to behave as a local carpenter should. It is not always easy to step away from expectations that keep us in a little box. Jesus didn't perform miracles there because the people were stuck in a narrow view of the world and its possibilities.

Thursday
Mark 6:7–13

'He ordered them to take nothing for their journey ...'

Jesus sent his friends out in pairs. He knew the value of companionship. Indeed, his life would include experiences of loneliness. His message seems to be that people may not accept you but at least you can accept each other. With whom will you step out to undertake today's journey?

Friday
Mark 6:14–29

'... he was greatly perplexed ...'

Herod found himself in a dreadful predicament. He was infatuated with the daughter of Herodias, whose name we never learn. He swore an oath and, as a result, was forced either to be humiliated or to have John the Baptist killed. John was the opposite of Herod. He knew where he stood and what mattered. Every new day presents us with this choice. Do we make deliberate choices, or are we pushed around by impulses?

Saturday
Mark 6:30–34

'... they were like sheep without a shepherd ...'

Jesus wanted to rest with his friends and hear their stories. But his compassion for the crowd changed things. It is not easy to get this balance right. We need time on our own with God. We are also called to respond heart and soul to the needs of people in our lives. Perhaps we can ask God to meet us when we feel lost, 'like sheep without a shepherd'.

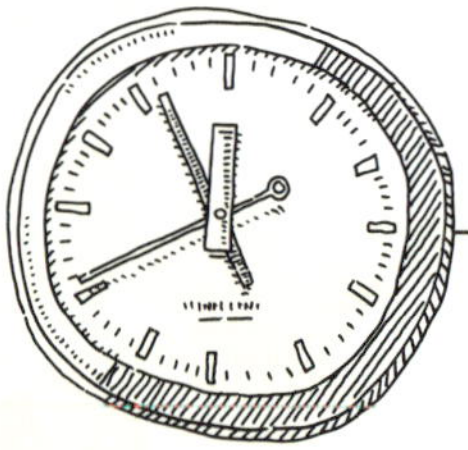

Week 5

We are all lifelong learners. The Holy Spirit is our teacher. This week we are reminded that teaching and learning happen in many different ways. The gospel readings come from a section we might call the schoolroom of Mark's Gospel. Let's make sure we are paying attention. The teaching of Jesus will make our lives richer if we truly understand it. Life can be testing, but here are some of the answers. They will feed our true hunger.

Prayer for Week 5

God of my confusion, Thank you for listening to me and my problems. Help me to find the simplicity of heart to which our faith calls us and to trust you to help me understand even hard lessons. Amen.

Monday
Mark 6:53–56

'... people at once recognized him ...'

People followed Jesus because they were fragile and needy. Let's pause today and ask ourselves about our own needs. Even if we start the day by visiting the gym or walking the dog, there is a sense in which we are all on stretchers, needing others to help us, needing God's love and grace to grow. Where do we really hope to meet God today? How will we respond to the Lord?

Tuesday
Mark 7:1–13

'... some of his disciples were eating with defiled hands ...'

We might not squabble about washing our hands. We know it is a good thing to do before eating. But we surely recognize the manipulative behaviour of the scribes and Pharisees who are quite happy to twist their tradition to their own advantage, 'making void the word of God.' God calls us to faith, not power.

Wednesday
Mark 7:14–23

'All these evil things come from within, and they defile a person.'

It is great when Jesus uses the language of the street. He said that food goes into us from outside and ends up in the sewer. It does not go into our hearts. On the other hand, what comes from our hearts will make or break our relationship with God. Our hearts are the fields in which our faith grows. Let us always listen to what St. Mary MacKillop called 'the whisperings of God' in our hearts.

Thursday
Mark 7:24–30

'For saying that, you may go ...'

The Syrophoenician woman may have had just a cameo, but she is one of the great characters in the gospels. A port such as Tyre is a melting pot of diversity. Jesus was tired. Did he really refer to this forceful woman as a 'dog'? She confronted him, and Jesus backed down. After all, she was standing up for her daughter. For whom will we stand up today? From where will our strength come?

Friday
Mark 7:31–37

'They were astounded beyond measure ...'

We use the word *ephphatha* ('be opened') when someone is baptized. Why? There is a sense in which we are all tied up or blocked. We pray that our ears will be opened to hear God's word and our tongue able to proclaim it. The scene in today's gospel is physically intimate: Jesus put his own spit on the man's tongue. Our encounter with God is like that. This day, God's word will be spoken in our lives and in creation. How can we be sure to hear it?

Saturday
Mark 8:1–10

'I have compassion for the crowd ...'

Jesus must have been a compelling teacher. The crowds were with him for three days and seemed to forget about eating to the extent that Jesus was worried they might collapse on the way home. These days, there would be food caravans following as well. Jesus started with the resources his friends had with them: seven loaves. He will start with our resources today and use them to meet the hunger of others. What might those resources be?

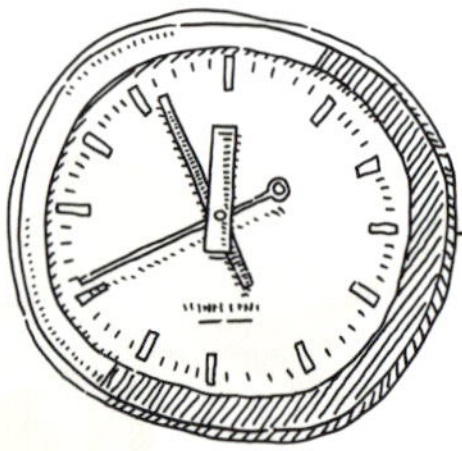

Week 6

I was 14 when I received my first pair of glasses. I can still remember the experience. The world looked fresh and new. Many years later, the same thing happened when I had my cataract surgery. This week, Mark's Gospel presents us with breathtaking visions. Faith is like a pair of glasses. It can help us see things clearly. The same thing happens when somebody creates a beautiful painting that transforms a mundane object, such as a railway bridge. Faith helps us see in colour.

Prayer for Week 6

God of my glasses, Help me to see the world as you see it and to notice the small signs of your grace, which saves us from our being stuck just with ourselves. Amen.

Monday
Mark 8:11–13

'Why does this generation ask for a sign?'

Jesus was annoyed that people were always asking for a sign from heaven. He was more than annoyed. A sigh came straight from his heart. He was fed up. People want thunder and lightning. They need to learn to look at the world around them with all its needs and all its possibilities. Perhaps this week we can look in the right direction and notice the signs God is already holding.

Tuesday
Mark 8:14–21

'Watch out ...'

Jesus' friends give us all hope. They never seem to catch on. Jesus asked them to keep their eyes open, and they concluded, 'It is because we have no bread'. They were so obtuse. 'Do you have eyes and fail to see?' Few of us are much wiser. We react to things from day to day. God calls us to see a bigger picture.

Wednesday
Mark 8:22–26

'Can you see anything?'

It takes a while for the man in today's gospel to see things clearly. At first, people look like walking trees. Eventually, they come into focus. The story reminds us that faith is a journey. God works with us. But it takes time. Deep faith does not expect instant results. It is more open than that.

Thursday
Mark 8:27–33

'You are setting your mind not on divine things ...'

Jesus saw what was coming, and it wasn't pleasant, yet it was at the heart of his identity. That is why he asked his friends who they thought he was. The answer was that he was the one whose relationship with God would lead to suffering and death and then to new life. This is the Christian story. We are mostly like Peter. We wish suffering didn't have to happen, least of all to us.

Friday
Mark 8:34 – 9:1

'... what can they give in return for their life?'

What are our crosses? How are we called to lose our lives? They are radical questions. Every day of a Christian's life demands an element of sacrifice, of surrender to God's plan. Think back to yesterday. When were we called to renounce ourselves and take up our crosses?

Saturday
Mark 9:2–13

'... it is good for us to be here ...'

Our world is transfigured every day. When we encounter a person in pain and refuse to see only their grief or anguish – instead we see their dignity as a child of God, loved and supported by grace. It is good for us to be there. It is good for us to encounter Christ as we look with compassion on a world of endless possibility.

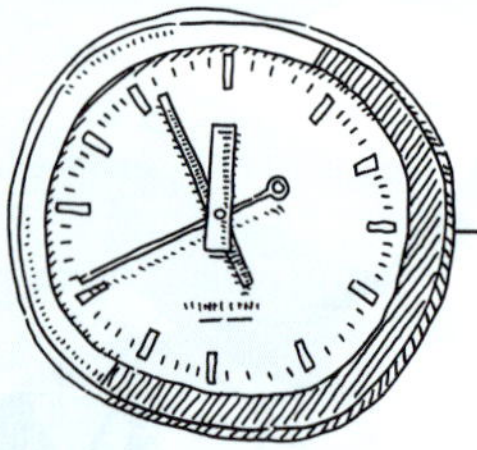

Week 7

In so many ways, my life keeps getting better. One reason is that I try to keep it simple. This applies especially to faith. There are many interesting books to read and podcasts to hear. But when I sit down each day with the Lord, even for a short time, I am more likely just to breathe a deep sigh of relief. 'Here I am, Lord. Help me to live this day as you would like.' I ask the Lord to take my anxiety and worry. These are my worst temptations. I ask that they be replaced by gratitude.

Prayer for Week 7

God of my daily grind, Open my eyes to wonder, my mouth to laugh, my hands to hold, my feet to follow, for this day is yours, not mine, and you are always up to something. Amen.

LOVE
WINS

Monday
Mark 9:14–29

'Help my unbelief!'

It sounds like the boy in today's gospel might be autistic. He is unable to speak. He throws himself into fire and water, desperate for stimuli from the outside world. No wonder the father is confused. He prays, 'I believe. Help my unbelief!' It is the perfect prayer, humble and honest. We could all share it.

Tuesday
Mark 9:30–37

' ... they did not understand ...'

As Mark's Gospel continues to work its way into the marrow of our bones, Jesus returns over and over to his coming ordeal. The disciples didn't understand. They were arguing about which one was the greatest. Before we scoff at them, we might consider ourselves. Even the best of us can find our ego getting between ourselves and God. We ask, 'What's in it for me?' Better to ask, 'Who's in it with me?'

Wednesday
Mark 9:38–40

'... because he was not following us ...'

Jesus didn't believe in too many fences or walls. If someone was trying to help others in his name, they were part of his community. 'Whoever is not against us is for us.' When push comes to shove, not many people are against us. We can be too defensive. We need to trust that God is at work in every life, not just our own.

Thursday
Mark 9:41–50

'... everyone will be salted with fire.'

'Have salt in yourselves, and be at peace with one another.' What might Jesus have meant by these beautiful words? Perhaps they were an invitation to add relish to the world. To enrich the flavour of life for others. To make the great banquet of life more inviting.

Friday
Mark 10:1–12

'... from the beginning of creation... '

At a time when women had few rights, Jesus taught that they couldn't just be tossed aside because a man made a writ of dismissal. He believed heart and soul that relationships should be based on justice, especially relationships with those closest to us. Intimacy is about far more than clever lawyers.

Saturday
Mark 10:13–16

'Let the little children come to me ...'

Children create the most wonderful drawings of God. They are colourful and imaginative, unconstrained by all the complexities that occur to the minds of adults. Jesus invites us to welcome the kingdom of God like a child: full of excitement and anticipation. Ready for any kind of fun.

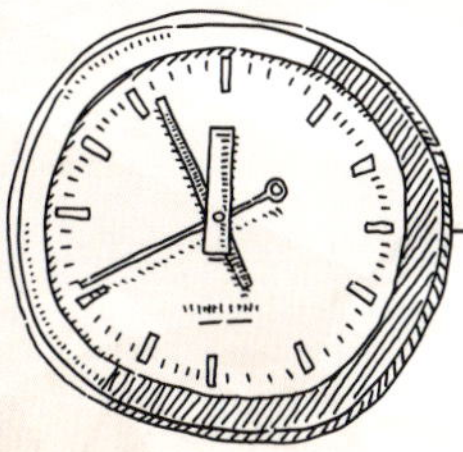

Week 8

By the end of this week, Mark's Gospel will have brought us to Jerusalem and to the horrifying events that Jesus has long anticipated. There is a real sense of journey in Mark's story. We know where it is leading. Yet, the characters we meet along the way are both fascinating and challenging. Jesus stopped many times. No matter what was coming up, he was fully alive in the present moment and responsive to the needs of others. He gave them his undivided attention. This is the life faith asks of us. Every day is a fresh gift.

Prayer for Week 8

God of unsealed roads, Some days we travel through dust, others through mud, sometimes through beautiful, open country, sometimes with others, other times alone. Guide our journey; bring us home. Amen.

Monday
Mark 10:17–27

'You lack one thing ...'

Someone once said that true faith is what you have when you have nothing else left. The rich young man did not understand this. He even saw his religious observance as a kind of possession: he had kept all the rules. In Mark's Gospel, it says that Jesus looked at him with love. The man had no idea how tangled up he has become. Jesus asked him to let go. He asks us the same thing.

Tuesday
Mark 10:28–31

'Many who are first will be last ...'

The word 'leaving' sums up this week's gospel readings. Jesus said that leaving everything behind is the only way to truly arrive. Each day renews that invitation.

Wednesday
Mark 10:32–45

'... it is not so among you ...'

You have to wonder about James and John. Jesus chose them to accompany him to the top of the mountain, where they saw him transfigured. Since then, he reminded them several times that they were on the road to Calvary. They just didn't get the message. They wanted positions of honour and prestige. All of us are inclined to worry about our status. Jesus calls us to be the least.

Thursday
Mark 10:46–52

'Jesus, Son of David, have mercy on me.'

Timaeus was beautiful. He couldn't see, but he certainly had his voice. When people told him to be quiet, he called all the louder. He wouldn't be bullied. Nearing Jerusalem, Jesus still focused on the needs of others. He said, 'What do you want me to do for you?' Let's take a few moments today to hear Jesus ask us the same question.

Friday
Mark 11:11–26

'... my house shall be called a house of prayer.'

Mark can be savage. Today, he notes that the fig tree had withered 'right down to the roots'. Jesus seems to treat the tree harshly. The important thing is that we are called to be swept up in the drama of life and death. Jesus is angry when people choose plastic lives. 'My house shall be called a house of prayer for all the nations.' We must decide if that means us or if we, like the traders, are just there for our own advantage.

Saturday
Mark 11:27–33

'... we do not know.'

Jesus could smell fear. Maybe it was because he was justifiably apprehensive about the coming trauma. It didn't take long for him to uncover the anxiety of the chief priests and scribes. They wanted to defend their narrow system of belief. Jesus wants us to let down our defences and allow God close to our hearts.

Week 9

This week is the last one in Ordinary Time that we spend with Mark's Gospel. Jesus comes across several people whose life is built around a single word. That word is 'no'. The tenants in the vineyard say no. The hypocrites say no. The Sadducees say no to eternal life. The only one who really says 'yes' is the widow who gives two small coins. Her response to life speaks more powerfully than all the rest. Faith in God asks us to embrace life in a positive way. It means saying yes to God every day as we embrace whatever comes our way, strange or familiar, comforting or confronting.

Prayer for Week 9

God of green salad, Help us take pleasure in simple things, not to overload ourselves with heavy food, least of all the stodgy ideas of the religious authorities from the time of Jesus. Help us to follow you lightly, lovingly, with grams of hope, not kilograms of worry. Amen.

NO
SWIMMING
NO
BOATING
NO
DOGS

Monday
Mark 12:1–12

'... the stone that the builders rejected...'

We all have experiences of rejection, even if it is just a forgotten anniversary or a boss who can't say thank you. The story of the tenants reminds us that these tough times can become the keystone for something else that is 'the Lord's doing'. Maybe that something is a greater compassion for others who are pushed to the side.

Tuesday
Mark 12:13–17

'Whose head is this?'

Jesus asked about the picture on a coin. It is an image of Caesar, the emperor. None of us has that kind of power. Instead, we are all the *imago dei*, the image of God. We all have wonderful gifts to share.

Wednesday
Mark 12:18–27

'He is God not of the dead, but of the living.'

There are plenty of people who spend their lives like the Sadducees. They like catching people out, using passive aggression to diminish others. They use penny-pinching questions when God asks them to have an open heart. They don't really live. Jesus was brilliant with them. The Lord is God of the living. Perhaps today we can be outlandish in love.

Thursday
Mark 12:28–34

'... you are not far from the kingdom of God.'

It's a pity that love is trivialized. You meet people who love their shoes, their car, their fine wine. It's great to appreciate those things. Jesus spoke of loving God 'with all your heart, with all your soul, with all your mind, with all your strength'. It is a holistic experience. It leaves nothing in reserve.

Friday
Mark 12:35–37

'... Sit at my right hand ...'

The people were delighted by what Jesus said in the temple. He clearly touched a raw nerve. How? Yet again, he brought down a barrier, namely the idea that those descended from David have a special standing in the eyes of God. We are all invited to sit close to the Lord.

Saturday
Mark 12:38–44

'... she ... has put in everything ...'

The widow in today's gospel only had a few lines, yet she is one of the most memorable characters in the whole of Scripture. We even use the expression 'the widow's mite' to speak of a small contribution that cuts close to the bone. Jesus saw her heart and was encouraged by her example. He will be like her, giving everything he possesses.

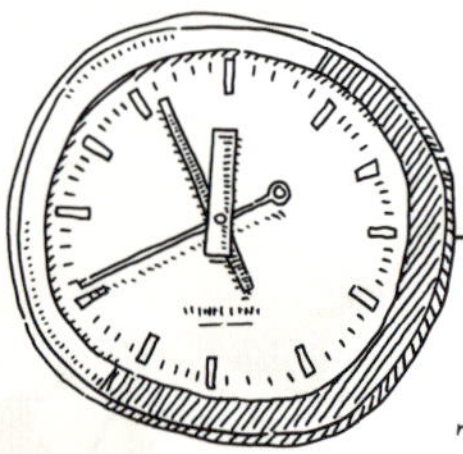

Week 10

This week we begin our time with Matthew's Gospel, embarking upon the so-called Sermon on the Mount. Perhaps this sermon is a compilation of many things Jesus said in different times and places. It hardly matters. Chapter 5 of Matthew's Gospel is one of the greatest and most radical collections of teaching in human history. It is a work of art that waters our roots and asks us to grow, blossom and spread our branches. There are some challenging words here, but they all serve to help us truly flourish.

Prayer for Week 10

God of our mouths, Help us find the right words for today, not borrowed words, or angry words, or slippery words, or lazy words. May our words be like the clothes we choose to greet the world, showing our best selves, responsive to the weather of the day. Amen.

Monday
Matthew 5:1–12

'Blessed are the pure in heart ...'

Blessed really means happy. Throughout history, hundreds of thinkers have offered the recipe for happiness. Few of them are as raw and truthful as the beatitudes. They call us to deep peace and contentment in the midst of our living and equally deep longing for what is right.

Tuesday
Matthew 5:13–16

'You are the salt of the earth.'

Let your light shine! This doesn't invite us to be arrogant or boastful or self-promoting. Heaven knows we soon tire of people like that. The light shines for everyone in the house. In other words, for others. There is nothing godly about denying our gifts, especially denying them for the service of others.

Wednesday
Matthew 5:17–19

'I have come ... to fulfill.'

In Matthew's Gospel, Jesus was very appreciative of his Jewish tradition. He loved the law of Moses in which, as a young person, he discovered God and learned how to live. At the same time, he urged people not to get trapped in the fine print of 'a tithe of mint and dill'. He endorsed the 'purpose of the law', which is the daily discovery of God and surrender to grace.

Thursday
Matthew 5:20–26

'... first be reconciled with your brother or sister ...'

The sign of peace at Mass is more than symbolic. Before we go to the altar, we remember God's call to be peacemakers. Hopefully, we take this into our daily lives, courageously working through issues with people in a gentle and positive spirit. Jesus knows that anger can be poison.

Friday
Matthew 5:27–32

'But I say to you: ...'

Jesus believes in integrity. Of course, we need to behave in appropriate ways. Jesus calls us to look deeper: at what is happening in our hearts. He doesn't really expect us to commit acts of self-harm. On the contrary, self-love involves having some control over the secret traffic through our minds and hearts.

Saturday
Matthew 5:33–37

'Let your word be "Yes, Yes ..."'

Many workplaces speak of 'controlling the narrative' and 'staying on message'. This is the world in which words are bought and sold. They are more part of marketing than open truth-telling. Jesus said to let your yes be yes and your no be no. In other words, we should inhabit what we say, in plain, honest and genuine words.

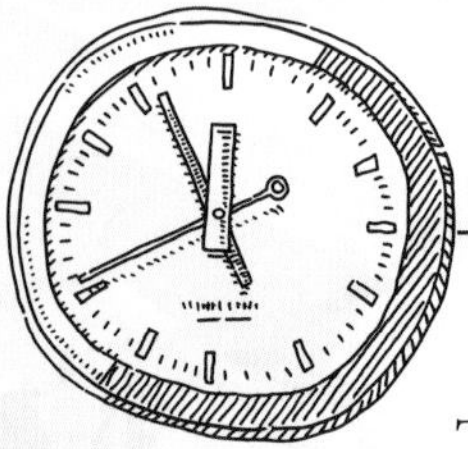

Week 11

The Sermon on the Mount is possibly the greatest collection of wisdom teaching in human history. Certainly, for Christians the words and images of Jesus continue to surprise and challenge us day in and day out. This week, we are asked to ponder the connection between the way we pray and the way we live. Jesus also asks us not to be the prisoners of our culture or our history. He uses phrases such as 'you have learned how it was said' or 'don't be the same as certain people'. Jesus calls us to be different. It's not always easy.

Prayer for Week 11

God of all Google, We use search engines to find many things. We look for tips and facts, maps and instructions. We also search for inspiration and words of wisdom. May we remember that the Word was made flesh and dwelt among us, and that Jesus never uploaded his message but shared it with friends, as he shares it with us. Amen.

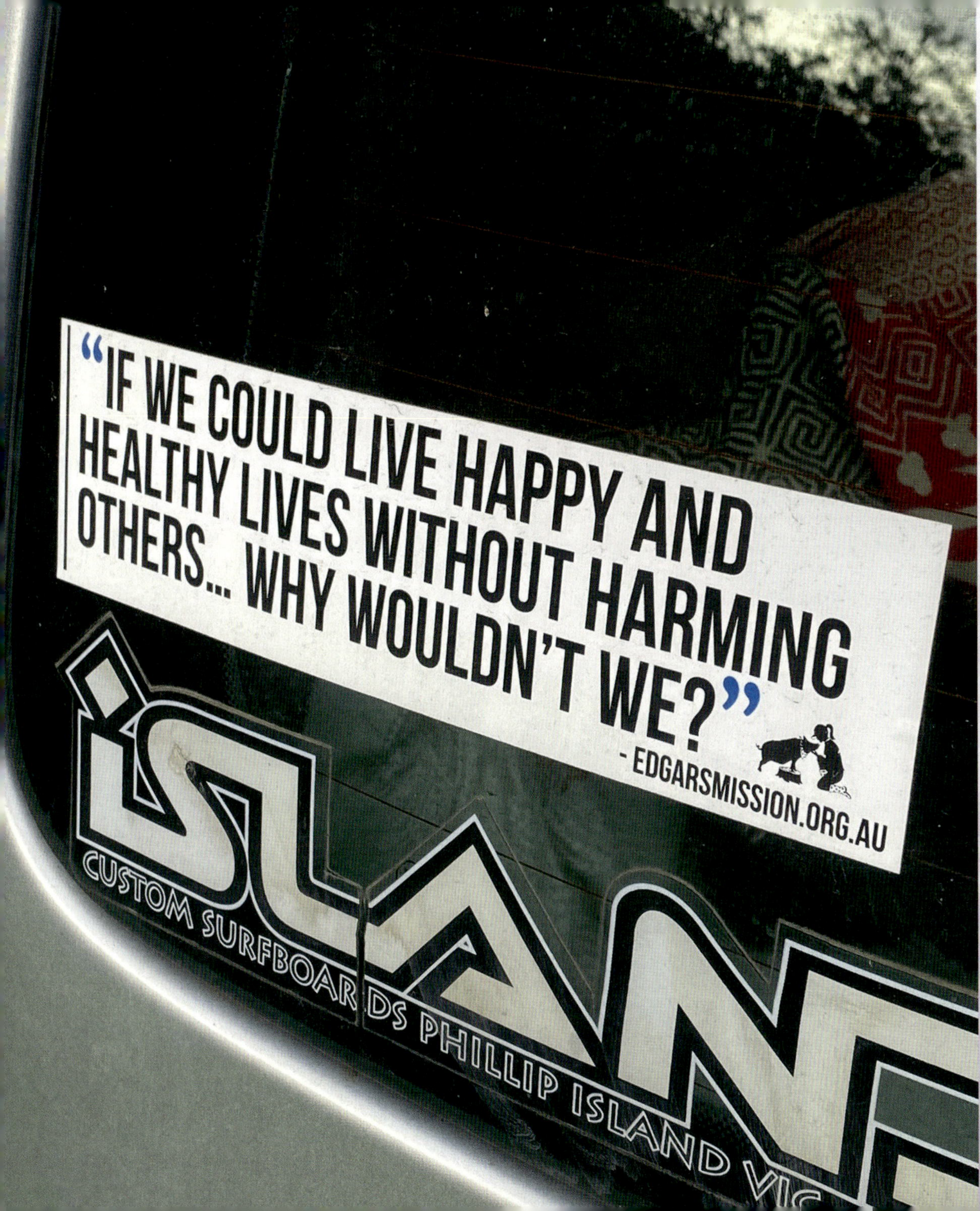
"IF WE COULD LIVE HAPPY AND
HEALTHY LIVES WITHOUT HARMING
OTHERS... WHY WOULDN'T WE?"
- EDGARSMISSION.ORG.AU
CUSTOM SURFBOARDS PHILLIP ISLAND VIC

Monday
Matthew 5:38–42

'Give to everyone who begs from you ...'

Jesus tells us to offer the other cheek. Immediately, we start thinking of all the conflict zones in the world. If only somebody could be the first to break the cycle of violence and destruction. These words also come home to us personally. Jesus tells us that relationships are more important than winning. If someone has taken advantage of us, are we really going to give them our shirt as well? With whom will we walk an extra mile today?

Tuesday
Matthew 5:43–48

'... love your enemies ...'

Jesus offered a vision for the entire world. He said that the same rain falls on everyone, regardless of what we may have done or the type of people we are. We have all met perfectionists. Often, they want to control the world and end up living defensive lives. When Jesus asks us to be perfect in the way that God is perfect, he is thinking of the opposite. He asks us to let go of our defences. It's OK for us to be imperfect because God is perfect.

Wednesday
Matthew 6:1–6, 16–18

'... your Father who sees in secret ...'

Where is your secret room, the place that you can meet God in private? A place for an intimate relationship that doesn't need spectators or commentators? For some it is the front seat of the car as they wait to collect their children. For others it is a park or garden. For most of us, it varies. God nudges a way into every life. It will happen today if we care to notice.

Thursday
Matthew 6:7–15

'... hallowed be your name ...'

We all love the words of the Lord's Prayer, also called the Our Father. There is good reason for this. It links together the awesome nature of God with our own need for both food and forgiveness. Many saints have urged us to take the prayer phrase by phrase and really ponder its depths. At the same time, Jesus said to pray like this. In other words, he suggests we find ways to build bridges of our own between our needs and God's vision.

Friday
Matthew 6:19–23

'Do not store up for yourselves treasures on earth ...'

Think for a moment of the things you are planning to do today. It might be quite a list. Hopefully it will include talking with friendly people. Jesus reminds us of the importance not just of what we do but of the attitude we bring to it. The light, he said, is inside us. It would be dreadful if 'the light in you is darkness'. We are called to bring a positive and hopeful spirit to the day.

Saturday
Matthew 6:24–34

'Today's trouble is enough for today.'

We all get anxious. Possibly we are anxious about something today. Jesus had practical advice. He said, 'do not worry about tomorrow'. In other words, let us live this day. It is a unique gift. Jesus reminds us that we are part of creation. We all have a special place in nature. Too much worry can blind us to that.

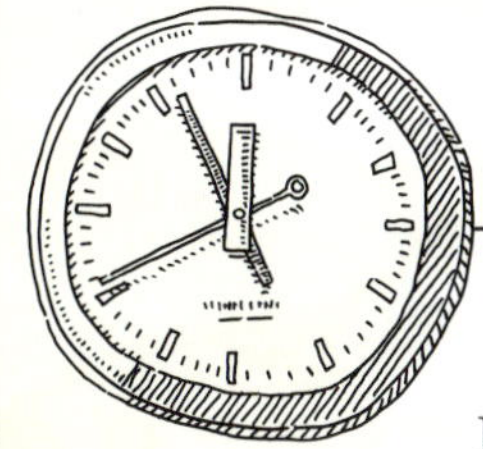

Week 12

Have you ever seen an old sign on a shop or a wall, a survivor from a previous life? Some people call them ghost signs. They remind us that we are not the first people to walk this way. There were others before us through countless generations. Their traces can still be found if we take time to appreciate them. This week, we spend more time with the Sermon on the Mount from Matthew's Gospel. So much of Jesus' teaching is present beneath the layers of our culture. Sometimes it is a bit like a sign that has almost vanished in the rush to create things that look brighter and shinier. Christians often remind themselves and each other that the words of Jesus have stood the test of time. Our lives can make them easier to see beneath the mad rush of ambition and self-interest.

Prayer for Week 12

God of compassion, Be with us when we lack energy, when we are tired or frustrated, when we wish the meeting would end, or the train would arrive, or our children would call. Teach us to be kind to ourselves and patient with others, able to see something good in everyone. Amen.

ALEX BARFOOT
SHOE REPAIRS
SURGICAL FOOTWEAR
22

Monday
Matthew 7:1–5

'First take the log out of your own eye ...'

We live in such a judgmental world. So many people have harsh words for each other. Few take time to really understand people who see things differently. 'The measure you give will be the measure you get.' Jesus asks us to be generous in the way we think of each other, even people we don't know. His words are more relevant now than ever before.

Tuesday
Matthew 7:6, 12–24

'... do to others as you would have them do to you ...'

Today's gospel says a lot about self-respect. Jesus asks us not to throw our pearls in front of pigs, to treat others as we would like to be treated and to make the difficult choices that lead to life. Taken together, these sayings ask us to value the good things God has entrusted to us, even if others don't value them. We are grateful for gifts that others may not even notice.

Wednesday
Matthew 7:15–20

'Thus you will know them by their fruits.'

There's an old saying that it takes years to become an overnight success. Jesus reminds us that the decisions we make on the spur of the moment are the work of a lifetime. 'A good tree cannot bear bad fruit.' Day by day, the work of grace in our lives helps us to grow and spread our branches with love and confidence.

Thursday
Matthew 7:21–29

'... the crowds were astounded at his teaching ...'

There are plenty of so-called spiritual experts around, people who are happy to sell courses or subscriptions of one kind or another. Jesus knew that we are vulnerable at the level of our souls. It is easy to be exploited. He finished his extraordinary sermon with the reminder that those who listen to his words and put them into practice are like those who build their houses on rock, not sand.

Friday
Matthew 8:1–4

'Lord, if you choose, you can make me clean.'

In Jesus' time, a person with diseases such as the man Jesus encountered in today's gospel led a lonely life. This is still the case, especially for those who live with disability, mental health issues or old age. Jesus reached into that loneliness. 'I do choose,' he said. He reaches past our defences as well.

Saturday
Matthew 8:5–17

'... I am not worthy to have you come under my roof ...'

The centurion was a figure of power, an authority of the empire that occupied Jesus' homeland. Yet, he cared enough about his servant, a person of much lower status, to approach Jesus for help. He related to Jesus through his own understanding of life: he was used to being obeyed. We all meet Jesus in the same way, formed by our lives, relationships and the work we have done. Jesus meets us in our own reality and transforms it.

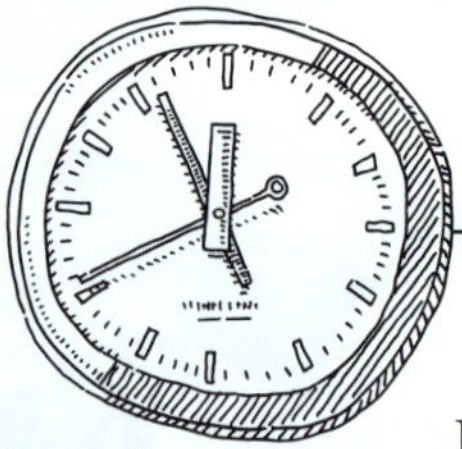

Week 13

Jesus showed the path of life. He often did this by entering into unexpected and wonderful relationships, characterized by both tenderness and honesty. This week, the stories from Matthew's Gospel are full of memorable characters: the disciples in the boat, the two men full of demons, a child with paraplegia, the tax collector and even the Pharisees. Jesus knew them all. They all had names. Their humanity was like names left in wet concrete: it wasn't washed away by life's circumstances, no matter how challenging those could be. What kind of relationship is God trying to develop with us this week?

Prayer for Week 13

God of our homecoming, We thank you for the close of each day, a quiet moment in our familiar space. We thank you for the objects on our walls and shelves that remind us we have walked far together, you and I. We thank you for a warm bed on a cold night, or an open window on a hot one. We give thanks for stillness, the well from which we draw tomorrow's energy. Amen.

Monday
Matthew 8:18–22

'... the Son of Man has nowhere to lay his head.'

It is fascinating how many connections the gospel writers make between Jesus and the natural world. Their stories are full of lakes, mountains, rivers, trees, birds, fish and seas. In today's gospel, Jesus says that he doesn't even have the security of foxes and birds. Following him may not even allow time to grieve those who have died. All we can do is trust in God's guidance.

Tuesday
Matthew 8:23–27

'Why are you afraid ...'

Jesus didn't have much use for fear. This is worth thinking about in a world that is riddled by anxiety. So many people are nervous of each other. The number of words that end in the suffix 'phobia' grows every year. When his friends were in a storm on the lake, they were afraid. This is significant, because these people had worked on the lake all their lives. 'Why are you afraid,' Jesus replied, 'you of little faith?'

Wednesday
Matthew 8:28–34

'What have you to do with us ...'

The story of the two men with severe mental illness living in isolation in the stone country is enough to touch any heart. It likely has even more of an impact on those of us with family and friends who live with the kind of anguish that alienates others. They are described as 'creatures so fierce that no one could pass that way'. Jesus brought them from loneliness into connection. There are two miracles here. The men were healed. So, too, was the community that could now accept them.

Thursday
Matthew 9:1–8

'Stand up and walk.'

Jesus came back to his own town and met a person who was paralyzed. The chances are that Jesus knew this person all his life. Perhaps they grew up together or their families knew each other. Nazareth was not a big place. Jesus did not keep people in the roles that had been assigned to them by life's circumstances. He enabled his friend to stand for himself and walk home.

Friday
Matthew 9:9–13

'I desire mercy, not sacrifice.'

I'm not sure, in today's gospel, if Matthew is writing about himself or someone else with the same name! Let's imagine that this is an autobiographical story. The story says, 'he got up and followed him.' So few words for such a life-changing experience! Maybe words escaped him. When we say 'I love you,' we are in the same territory: beyond words. There may have been good reason why Matthew cherished the words of Jesus: 'Those who are well have no need of a physician, but those who are sick.'

Saturday
Matthew 9:14–17

'... new wine is put into fresh wineskins ...'

Jesus was highly intuitive. It says elsewhere in Scripture that he didn't need to be told what people were like because he already knew 'what someone had in them.' It was the same when it came to special occasions. Our faith is never inflexible. It responds to whatever is happening around us: there are times for joy and times for sorrow. Times for old ways and times to try something new. Our faith helps us to read and understand the world.

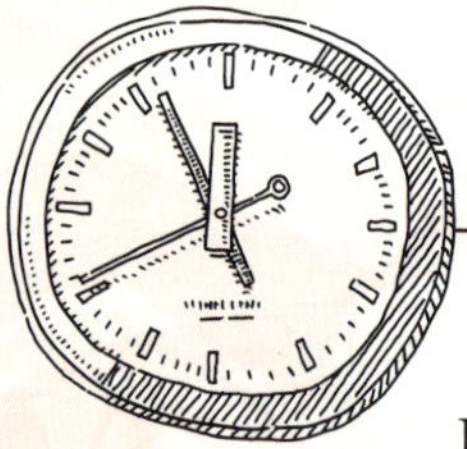

Week 14

It is great when we find a welcome on the mat. But it doesn't always happen. Sometimes there are things we have to say or do that invite a hostile response. We might think of friends who have spoken up against bullies in the workplace or others who have reminded thoughtless family members of their need to be kind to each other. We can think of people who have spoken up in defence of life or the environment or justice or equality. This week's gospel readings deal with the call to discipleship. Jesus made it clear that following him is by no means a soft option. Our faith certainly brings comfort and healing. It also calls us to courage.

Prayer for Week 14

God of our hands, Bless our efforts this day, help us to be makers not breakers, creators not fakers. May we be authentic, true to our calling, inspired by your example, alive to life's possibilities, wary of manipulation. Amen.

Bright & Bold
WELCOME
STRANGER

Monday
Matthew 9:18–26

'If I only touch his cloak ... '

Touch can be a beautiful gift. Our bodies are sensitive to the nearness of others. When this happens in the context of trust, we often feel the closeness of God at the same time. The woman in the story wanted to touch only Jesus' cloak. How and where are we reaching out to God today?

Tuesday
Matthew 9:32–38

'The harvest is plentiful, but the labourers are few ...'

Jesus felt compassion for people who were exhausted and depressed. They were 'like sheep without a shepherd.' We should give thanks to the people who brighten up our lives, especially those who provide insight and wisdom to help us understand things. At the same time, we can guarantee that we will be called this day to help someone who is a little lost in some way.

Wednesday
Matthew 10:1–7

'Jesus summoned his twelve disciples ...'

Imagine your name is on the list of disciples. Imagine Jesus including you among such heroes of faith as Peter, James and John. Where would Jesus send you?

Thursday
Matthew 10:7–15

'... the kingdom of heaven has come near.'

Jesus sent his friends out without any money or change of clothes. He told them to expect a welcome in some places and a rejection in others. Shaking the dust from their feet is an image of not carrying the burden of resentment, even if someone is unkind. Jesus asked them to keep going as well as they could. He asks the same of us. To keep trusting God.

Friday
Matthew 10:16–23

'... be wise as serpents and innocent as doves.'

Jesus asked his friends to be as 'wise as serpents and innocent as doves.' He asked them, even in the toughest times, not to worry about what they should say. 'It is not you who speak, but the Spirit of your Father speaking in you.' He is asking us not to let our ego get between people and God. We need the grace to surrender to a higher wisdom than ours.

Saturday
Matthew 10:24–38

'Are not two sparrows sold for a penny?'

Jesus said, 'nothing is covered up that will not be uncovered'. He wants us to be honest with God and with each other. We all create an image of ourselves. In business this is called a 'personal brand'. God loves us for who we really are in our depths. 'You are of more value than many sparrows.'

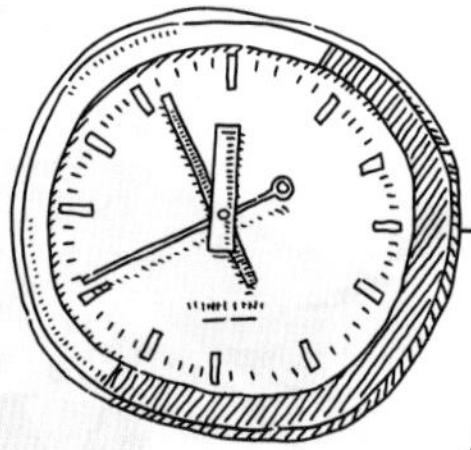

Week 15

A terrific Scripture scholar, Fr. Brendan Byrne, has written a commentary on Matthew's Gospel – *Lifting the Burden: Reading Matthew's Gospel in the Church Today*. He says he came to love this gospel later in life.

> 'In Matthew I discovered a gospel that teaches us to look at humanity through the eyes of Jesus and see it as afflicted and weighed down with all manner of burdens. Far from adding to humanity's burdens, Jesus comes to bear and lift them.'

It is good to remember those words this week when we encounter some of the most strident words in the whole New Testament. Some of those words are comforting, others are disturbing. All of them draw us into an honest relationship with God in which we can hand over our burdens. Brendan Byrne says:

> 'We would not read the Gospel of Matthew at all if we did not in some sense recognise that it is "our story" too.'

Prayer for Week 15

God of our burden, Help us to put down our baggage, look up from our phones, and set out with a lighter step on the road that you share with us. Amen.

oOh!
PROJECT COMPASSION
FOR ALL FUTURE GENERATIONS
Education can change her future
You can help
Project Compassion
Caritas AUSTRALIA
The Catholic agency for international aid and development

Monday

Matthew 10:34 – 11:1

'Do not think...'

'Those who lose their life for my sake will find it.' Jesus asks us to take up our crosses and follow him. It is curious that he spoke of the cross so long before he appeared before Pilate to be sentenced. He knew what awaited him. But he didn't stop teaching, however unwelcome his message. He continues teaching us this day.

Tuesday

Matthew 11:20–24

'... they would have repented ...'

Jesus was frustrated that so many places such as Tyre and Sidon, both port cities, were unable to take his message to heart and change their culture. Port cities are famously crowded and frenetic, a hotpot for the exchange of ideas. Perhaps the people were too busy even to notice Jesus. Sure enough, there may be signs of God's life that we are too preoccupied to notice.

Wednesday

Matthew 11:25–27

'All things have been handed over to me.'

Sometimes we can be too clever for our own good. There are other moments we enter with childlike simplicity, even if that means enjoying an ice cream or laughing at a silly joke. God asks us every day to enjoy the gift of life. My mother used to say that if we were having a tough day, we should just look at a flower.

Thursday

Matthew 11:28–30

'... I am gentle and humble in heart ...'

The words of today's gospel have been loved for centuries. 'Come to me ... and I will give you rest.' The Anglican *Book of Common Prayer* includes them in every celebration of the Eucharist. We all feel overburdened at times. We all need rest. God doesn't ask more than we can manage. God wants to share our burden.

Friday

Matthew 12:1–8

'Have you not read?'

On two occasions in Matthew's Gospel, Jesus uses the words from the prophet Hosea: 'I desire mercy and not sacrifice.' They indicate the path to life. Our acts of kindness allow grace to germinate in us. Compassion goes deeper than ritual.

Saturday

Matthew 12:14–21

'Here is my servant...'

Today's gospel presents us with Pharisees plotting to destroy Jesus. His response is to withdraw from the district. People can bring storms with them, too, and sometimes the best thing is to find a peaceful place with others you can trust. Despite the power of the Pharisees, the people followed Jesus. Everything about him was healing. The gospel uses words from the prophet Isaiah to describe him. He doesn't shout. He won't break the crushed reed; he won't put out the smouldering wick. In other words, he has a quiet respect for the weak. He makes space for them.

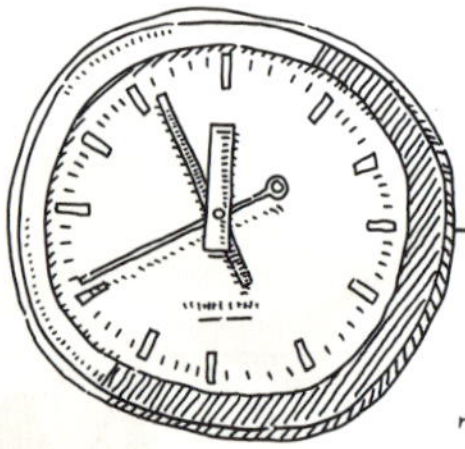

Week 16

There is a big difference between graffiti and vandalism. Surely we can think kindly of whoever was clever enough to take a sign that says 'Lease' and, with a few strokes of the pen, turn it into 'Love eases'. Why? Because on any plain day in the middle of the year, gestures of love make such a difference, even if it is simply someone who makes us a cup of tea and remembers exactly how we like it. This is the time of year when we recall Mary Magdalene. There are many myths and legends about her, few of them supported by Scripture. Her ability to accept the love of God eased the burden of her life. It gave her strength to share the message of the risen Lord.

Prayer for Week 16

God of the local park, We thank you for trees and people who walk their dogs. We thank you for sports teams and people jogging on their own. We thank you for someone else mowing the grass and all who care for your creation. May we be gardeners in your world, nurturing life from its roots to its branches. Amen.

Monday
Matthew 12:38–42

'... we wish to see a sign.'

There are plenty of signs in all our lives. We will see some in today's gospel and more tomorrow. Jesus referred to Solomon who, when a young king, was allowed to ask God for any gift. He requested wisdom. This was, indeed, a wise thing to do, suggesting that God often builds on the gifts we already have. We might ask for the wisdom to read the world and understand ourselves.

Tuesday
Matthew 12:46–50

'Whoever does the will of my Father in heaven.'

It is hard to accept that Jesus was so rude to his mother and brothers. His real point was that being close to God brings us into an intimate relationship. We are all members of God's family. He was not so much being unkind to his own family as challenging everyone else to be part of it.

Wednesday
Matthew 13:1–9

'A sower went out to sow.'

Jesus drew many stories from the natural world. He was close to creation and respected it. The stories of the fig tree, the mustard seed, the haul of fish and others remind us of the countless ways in which creation reveals the heart of the Creator. The same applies to the sower. We are called to be like rich soil, deep enough to allow the word of God to take root within us.

Thursday
Matthew 13:10–17

'To you it has been given to know the secrets of the kingdom of heaven ...'

Jesus explained that he used parables because the life of faith is full of mysteries. The use of imagination and stories helps us to explore those mysteries and understand with our hearts. Many saints were people of rich imagination and wonderful dreams. We, too, should enjoy the adventure of faith, often without knowing all the answers.

Friday
Matthew 13:18–23

'... such a person has no root, but endures only for a while ...'

After so many centuries, Jesus' description of the people who miss out on life is as vivid and relatable as ever. Some people are enthusiastic at first but have no staying power. Some are choked by worries, others by 'the lure of wealth'. Some lack depth. Some give up when the going gets tough. Jesus asks us to let our faith grow deep inside us.

Saturday
Matthew 13:24–30

'Let both of them grow together until the harvest ...'

Life is a mixed bag. The images of wheat and weeds growing together explains it beautifully. Both grow inside us: we all do saintly things as well as unkind ones. Yet, we often hang on to the callous and cruel things we may have done more than we appreciate the loving things. God will help us keep the good and burn the bad. God knows we are complex and helps us store in our hearts the memories that will assist us.

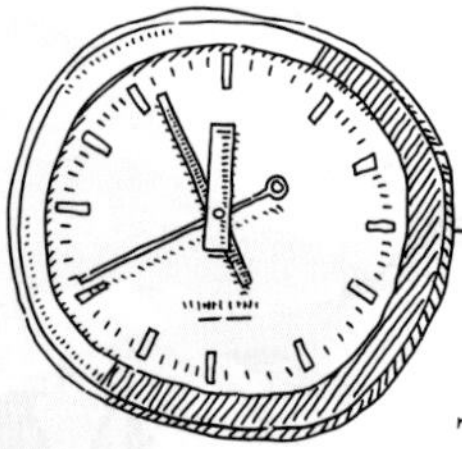

Week 17

There is a famous painting by Giambattista Tiepolo called *The Banquet of Cleopatra*. Never mind the fascinating story of how this enormous work, painted in the middle of the 18th century, ended up in the National Gallery of Victoria. You'd need a house the size of a castle if you owned it. At the centre, Cleopatra is poised to drop a priceless pearl into a flute of champagne in which, of course, the alcohol will dissolve it, like aspirin in water. Her gesture is one of wealth and power. She is portrayed as the centre of the world. If you wanted to represent everything Jesus was *not* talking about this week as he explained the kingdom of God, this image would be perfect.

The kingdom of God is not something any of us can own. It is the kind of pearl or treasure for which we need to keep looking; it is not one that we can keep under lock and key. There is no such thing as an arrogant Christian. We are all on a journey towards ever deeper humility.

Prayer for Week 17

God of all giving, We pray that for one day, we may stop asking and begin thanking you whose kingdom comes on earth as in heaven. Thank you for our daily bread, our daily forgiveness, our daily invitation. Amen.

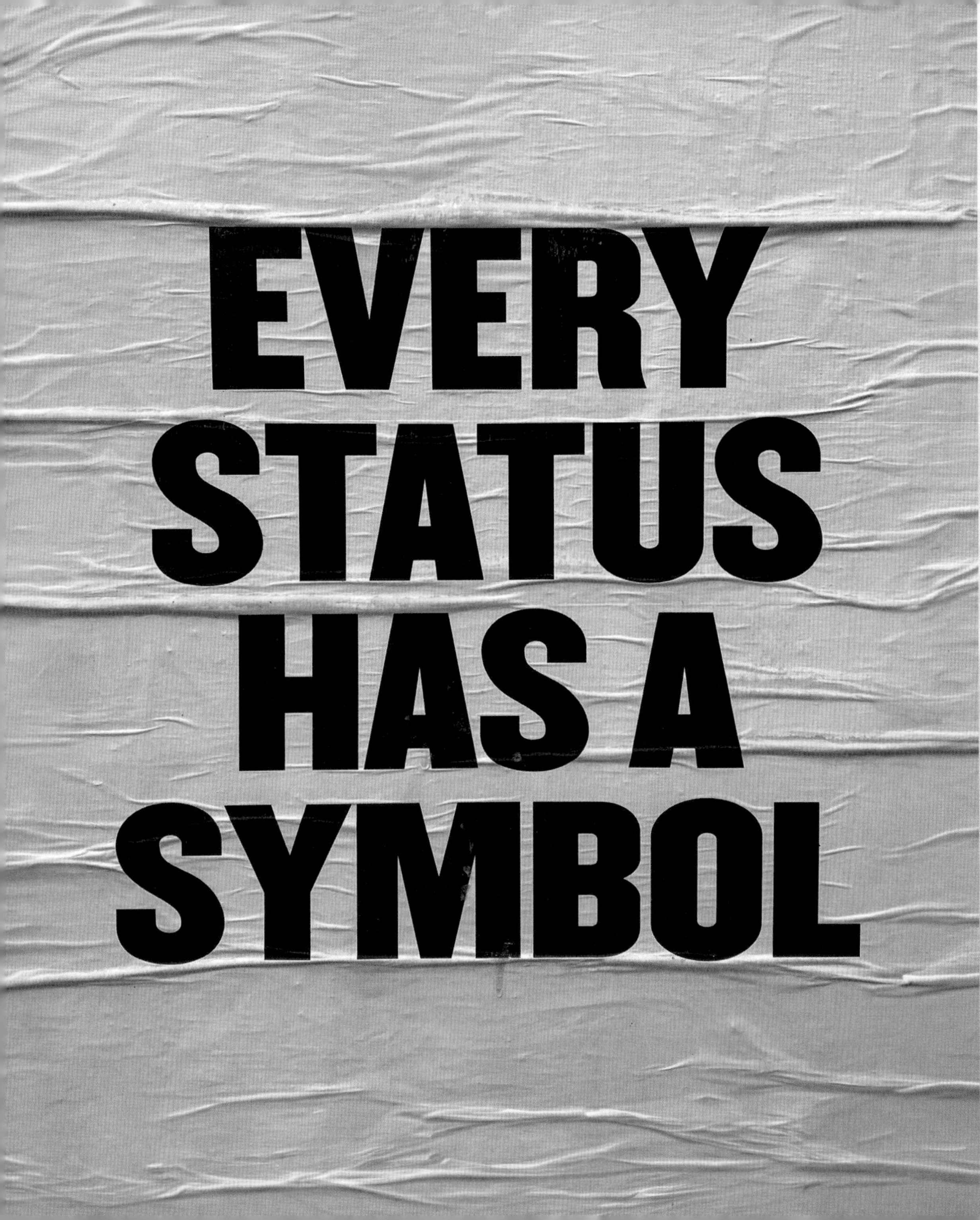
EVERY
STATUS
HAS A
SYMBOL

Monday
Matthew 13:31–35

'The kingdom of heaven is like a mustard seed…'

When speaking of a kingdom of truth and love, Jesus often used images from the natural world. If you have ever owned a bread maker or, better yet, made your own bread from scratch, you will know how little yeast is needed to raise the whole loaf. Our lives are like that. We are called to give the world a lift, not to let it down.

Tuesday
Matthew 13:36–43

'Let anyone with ears listen!'

We have often thought of the grinding of teeth as a sign of anguish. It is also the most common sleep disorder, known as bruxism. Being cut off from God is like the inability to properly rest. St. Augustine said, 'Our hearts are restless until they rest in you.' In God alone can we rest in peace.

Wednesday
Matthew 13:44–46

'The kingdom of heaven is like treasure hidden in a field.'

Coming up with an image to represent the kingdom of heaven can fire up the imagination. It is a treasure hidden in a field, a pearl of great price for which a merchant will sell everything. What images might we use in our day and age? The kingdom of heaven makes a Ferrari look like a go-kart. The kingdom of heaven makes a bottle of champagne seem like lemonade. It is like a person who chooses to live in a tent, not a mansion. Why don't we use our imagination to describe it? Jesus was always using his!

Thursday
Matthew 13:47–53

'… the kingdom of heaven is like a net …'

Dragnets have been banned in many parts of the world. They do too much damage to the ocean, capturing creatures that need to be protected as well as those that can be sold. They also haul in a lot of garbage, especially plastic, which has done so much damage to the marine environment. When you think about it, Jesus was saying that the kingdom of heaven will be like an ocean restored to its pristine condition. It will be like the world made whole.

Friday
Matthew 13:54–58

'Where did this man get this wisdom…'

Many of Jesus' experiences are familiar to us. He grew up in a small town, and the people there had him pigeon-holed to fill a certain position in life. 'Where did this man get this wisdom?' Jesus could slip out of the little box created for him, even if that meant he was rejected by people he had known all his life. We all face the same challenge. Our faith can take us beyond the script others have written for us.

Saturday
Matthew 14:1–12

'The king was grieved…'

Poignantly, the week concludes with the story of Herod, a man obsessed with image, reputation and status. He was manipulated by people he wanted to impress. Deep down, he was probably envious of John the Baptist, a figure of freedom and integrity. He was the kind of king who was so self-preoccupied that he couldn't begin to grasp what the kingdom of God might involve. It would turn all his beliefs upside down.

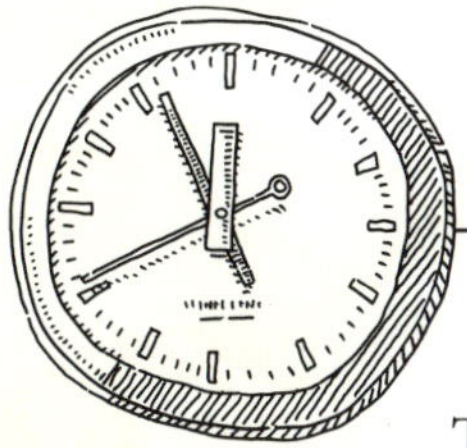

Week 18

There are many occasions in life when the words of the Psalms meet us exactly where we happen to find ourselves. How many times have we turned to the words, for example, 'O God, you are my God, I seek you, my soul thirsts for you' (Psalm 63). Or 'Have mercy on me, O God, according to your steadfast love; according to your abundant mercy blot out my transgressions' (Psalm 51). Or 'Where can I go from your spirit?' (Psalm 139). The Psalms have an uncanny ability to cut through the clutter and grime of so much of the world. Jesus knew them intimately, and they often seem to be in the background of his teaching. They helped him find courage to live out the demands of his unique relationship with the Father. Courage features in many of the gospels this week. Aristotle said that courage was a gateway virtue: no other virtue was possible without it. Our prayer calls us to courage.

Prayer for Week 18

God of our doubts, You call us across the water to get out of the boat, to leave our safe space, to discover you in our failings. May we remember the words of Psalm 33: 'Let your steadfast love, O Lord, be upon us, even as we hope in you.' Amen.

PSALM

Monday
Matthew 14:13–21

'We have nothing here but...'

Jesus must surely have been distressed by the news of the death of John the Baptist. He needed time to process what had happened, not least its implications for anyone such as himself who dared to speak against the powerful. Matthew places this moment beside the feeding of five thousand people. It is a poignant juxtaposition. Even in grief, we can still nurture others. Psalm 42 says, 'My tears have been my food ...'

Tuesday
Matthew 14:22–36

'Why did you doubt?'

We are all called, like Peter, to get out of our boats. To leave a safe place. To journey towards God, even if the Lord seems no clearer to us than a ghost. The Lord says, over and over, 'do not be afraid'. Isaiah 43 says, 'I have called you by name, you are mine.'

Wednesday
Matthew 15:21–28

'Great is your faith.'

The Canaanite woman is one of the most determined and courageous figures in the New Testament. Jesus even seems to compare her and her daughter to dogs. She wouldn't take no for an answer, and Jesus warmed to her strength of heart. Psalm 27 says, 'Wait for the Lord; be strong, and let your heart take courage...'

Thursday
Matthew 16:13–23

'... who do you say that I am?'

It can sometimes be difficult to take on board what God wants for us. This is surely the case with Peter in today's gospel. In one breath, he expressed the deepest discovery of his life: Jesus was 'the Son of the living God.' In the next breath, he was crestfallen because Jesus was so upfront about the journey he needed to undertake. Psalm 95 says, 'O that today you would listen to his voice!'

Friday
Matthew 16:24–28

'For those who want to save their life will lose it...'

We live in a culture that does not always understand or even respect big commitments. Relationships can be transient. Careers matter more than a calling. We buy clothes that don't last long and thus create a problem for the environment. When Jesus speaks about taking up our crosses to follow him, he is talking about the whole of our lives. Like any relationship, such a deep love needs to be renewed in the small details of every day. Psalm 25 says, 'Make me to know your ways, O Lord; teach me your paths.'

Saturday
Matthew 17:14–20

'... if you have faith the size of a mustard seed...'

Jesus confronted his friends because they didn't seem to have faith the size of a mustard seed. He might have said the same thing to any of us. We can all worry more about changing a light bulb than changing the light within us. Psalm 18 says, 'the Lord is my rock ... in whom I take refuge, my shield, and the horn of my salvation, my stronghold.'

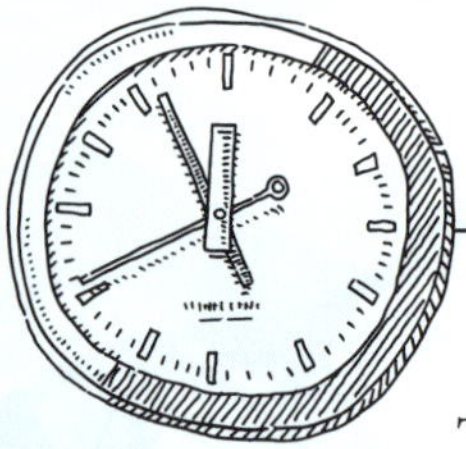

Week 19

This week, we ponder some of the words that have done a great deal to shape our idea of Christian community. 'Where two or three are gathered in my name, I am there among them.' 'How often should I forgive?'

On two occasions, Jesus tells us to become more like children. Perhaps he means full of wonder and awe. He also means more accepting. Why don't we try to enter this week in a spirit of acceptance, taking everything that comes as a gift from a loving Creator? We may not always understand the gift, but it is still given in love.

Prayer for Week 19

God of letting go, Help us to step away from painful memories, to open the door from the inside and set ourselves free. May we be agents of your grace in a world that needs healing and the ability to forgive. Lead us from the fire of our anger to a place near restful waters. Amen.

Monday
Matthew 17:22–27

'And they were greatly distressed.'

The story of Jesus using a coin that turns up in the mouth of a fish to pay his taxes is mystifying. It is the only time Jesus seems to perform a miracle in his own interests. There is a clue in the first few lines. Jesus knew he was about to be handed over to death. We have often heard that there are two certainties: death and taxes. For Jesus, the first of these offers a much closer walk with God.

Tuesday
Matthew 18:1–5, 10, 12–24

'... change and become like children.'

In Luke's Gospel, the Parable of the Lost Sheep is presented as a story of forgiveness, sitting close to the story of the lost coin and the two sons. In Matthew, it seems to be part of teaching about humility, part of the answer to the question 'Who is the greatest in the kingdom of heaven?' But surely these two experiences share a great deal. It takes humility both to seek and to give forgiveness. We are called to keep our lives in perspective.

Wednesday
Matthew 18:15–20

'... I am there among them.'

Pope Francis often talks about forgiveness. He knows that it isn't easy. Indeed, the very grace for which most people long eludes them – often because we live in a world that has lost any shared narrative of forgiveness and mercy. While legal remedies are important, they are hardly the same as mercy. Sometimes they can bind people in chains rather than set them free, as they truly hope. Pope Francis has described forgiveness as a 'basic human right'. He asks us to do all we can to release even people who have hurt us.

Thursday
Matthew 18:21 – 19:1

'... forgive your brother or sister from your heart.'

As always, today's gospel shows that Jesus has a profound understanding of human nature. We like to carry grudges and have power over others. When Jesus referred to forgiving somebody 'seventy-seven times', he was describing an entire lifestyle, one we are called to live 'from your heart'. Grace and mercy are the basics of our spiritual diet. They are not just for special occasions.

Friday
Matthew 19:3–12

'Let anyone accept this who can.'

There are always arguments about today's gospel, about divorce and eunuchs and so on. We have all been through broken relationships of one kind or another, and we all know people who have endured painful divorces. Jesus was not having a go at them, although he certainly spoke against men who treat women badly. He calls us to integrity and honesty in relationships. The love we have for others dates from the creation of the world. Our intimate lives are part of God's ongoing work of creation.

Saturday
Matthew 19:13–15

'... it is to such as these that the kingdom of heaven belongs ...'

One year, the most complaints a radio station received were not about politics or biased reporting. It was a broadcaster who announced at school pick-up time that Santa didn't exist. The phones ran hot. People, it seems, value the innocence of children. It's a pity we don't place the same value on the way children learn to pray and trust God. Let's do a little something today as a sign of our own trust.

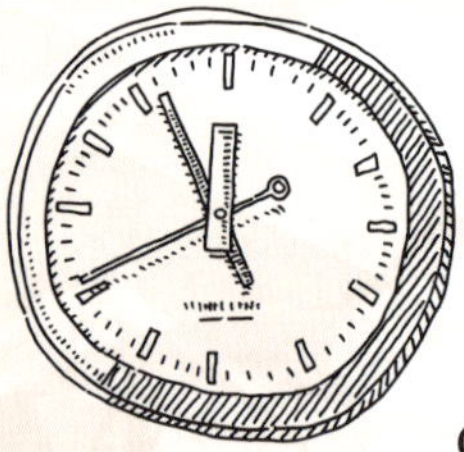

Week 20

Christianity is a way of looking at the world. It is a bit like this week's picture. Some people see a boring old electricity box. Someone else looks at the same thing and can see trees, fields, mountains and a homely place with a fire burning warmly. As Matthew's Gospel moves towards its appalling denouement in the death of Jesus, it focuses more and more on the extravagance of God. We encounter the stories of a rich young man, workers who only work an hour and a lavish wedding feast. Jesus puts the question to us: Can we be as exuberant in love as God is? Can we see the world in an open and loving way rather than a petty and self-serving way?

Prayer for Week 20

God of the impossible, We thank you for your extravagance, for your wild imagination, for your bleeding heart, all of which find a special place for us, and for the people who hurt us, and for the people we don't understand. Please meet us in this day and lift us beyond it. Amen.

SIGNAL FAULTS
WARNING
Irrigation · Turf · Seed · Lighting
Tanks · Pumps · Ponds

Monday
Matthew 19:16–22

'... what good deed must I do?'

We could all trade places with the rich young man. He thought he had done so well. You can almost hear the pride in his voice when he says, 'I have kept all these'. He might even have been fishing for a compliment when he asked, 'What do I still lack?' Jesus affirmed him, but not in the way he expected. In asking him to give everything to the poor and follow him, Jesus was expressing confidence that the man was capable of radical choices. We all are.

Tuesday
Matthew 19:23–30

'Many who are first will be last...'

Why do people strive to be rich? After all, there's only so much money you can spend. Jesus sees the downside of wealth. If your trust is in what you own, then your life is bound to be anxious and defensive. But if we can take to heart the words 'for God all things are possible', then we can find a freedom that means we don't have to be so self-reliant. Life is a journey, not a race.

Wednesday
Matthew 20:1–16

'Are you envious because I am generous?'

An old teacher once said to a graduating class that God would pursue them with love and grace until their dying breath. God never gives up on us. Prison chaplains, for example, often witness extraordinary journeys of faith and forgiveness. God is working at the start of the day, during the heat of the day and well past the eleventh hour.

Thursday
Matthew 22:1–14

'Go therefore into the main streets ...'

Have you heard the expression FOMO? It means 'fear of missing out', and it is a psychological pandemic. The irony is that people are so busy not missing out that they end up missing out. Today's gospel understands us very well. We are all preoccupied. It might be with farms and businesses or something else. We are invited to the banquet of life and sometimes leave before the main course.

Friday
Matthew 22:34–40

'This is the greatest and first commandment.'

The Pharisees observed hundreds of commandments. Jesus reduced them to the two main ones. This must have been confronting for Matthew because he loved the traditions of his people. Sometimes, however, we can be blinded by what people call BAU (Business As Usual). Jesus wants us to get down on our knees to check the foundations on which we build our lives: love of God and of each other.

Saturday
Matthew 23:1–12

'The greatest among you will be your servant.'

'Do whatever they teach you ... but do not do as they do.' This is a sad indictment. These days we would call it hypocrisy. We know, in modern language, that we must walk the talk. Be people of integrity, not image. We are called to speak our humble truth, not so much control the narrative or manipulate the messaging. Above all, we are called to lift burdens, not make them heavier. Humility makes space for others to grow.

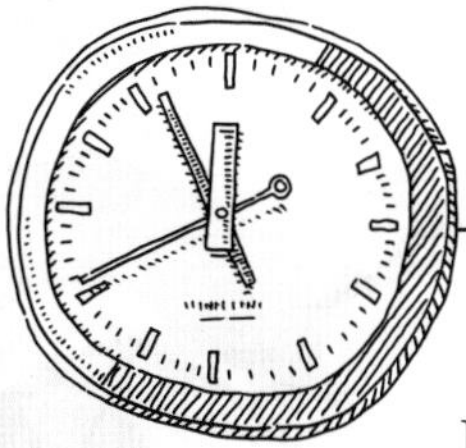

Week 21

I wonder what words we'd use these days instead of *alas*. You don't hear it much anymore. It is rather scornful. Perhaps we might say 'bad luck' or even something stronger. 'Get lost' or 'Clear out' all come to mind. Jesus uses the word 'alas' on numerous occasions in this week's gospel readings. It is easy to forget the extent to which he employed strong language. We remember all the kind things he said, and sure enough, there were far more of those. But he had no trouble speaking his mind, and he had no time for hypocrisy. There are times when we need to do some plain talking as well. We can be inclined to passive aggression, being nice to someone's face and criticizing them behind their backs. You always knew where Jesus stood. He believed in truth-telling more than controlling the narrative.

Prayer for Week 21

God of plain speaking, Help us find the right words this week: to build up, not tear down, to create trust, not break it, to comfort and also to challenge. Help us to find the right things to say to ourselves, to show ourselves love, but also to be honest with ourselves and not deceived by our own bland talk. Amen.

I MUST RESIST
I MUST RESIST
I MUST RESIST
I bought it.

Monday
Matthew 23:13–22

'... blind guides!'

Who were the scribes and Pharisees that annoyed Jesus so much? They were educated and faithful to their tradition. The problem was that they used their tradition to exclude people who may have been different. They made faith into an obstacle course. 'You lock people out of the kingdom of heaven.' These kinds of people still exist. We may even be a bit like this ourselves.

Tuesday
Matthew 23:23–26

'First clean the inside of the cup ...'

Jesus had a wonderful way with words. He was irritated by people who lost sight of what matters: 'You strain out a gnat but swallow a camel!' Gnats are like mosquitoes. Jesus gave the example of those who pay their religious tax on small herbs such as mint and dill but forget 'justice, mercy and faith'. They clean the outside of the cup for the sake of appearances but neglect the inside.

Wednesday
Matthew 23:27–32

'You are like whitewashed tombs ...'

When he was in full flight, Jesus was a force of nature. He couldn't abide those who worried about how things looked to others, people who spent their lives window dressing. He compared them to beautiful tombs that look great but are containers of death. He wants our minds and hearts to be alive, energized by our connection with God.

Thursday
Matthew 24:42–51

'Keep awake ...'

'The Son of Man is coming at an unexpected hour.' We don't know the precise time, but we know it will be today, and again tomorrow, and again the day after. The Lord comes to meet us in the people and events of the most ordinary day. We, in turn, are the means God uses to step into the lives of others. We just need to be awake to the daily love of God, standing ready for God to embrace us.

Friday
Matthew 25:1–13

'... you know neither the day nor the hour.'

Ten bridesmaids is a large number for one wedding. Jesus wasn't too concerned about the literal story he was telling but rather the point it was making. Having a lamp with no oil is like buying a flashlight but not the batteries. Both the oil and the batteries belong inside the lamp or flashlight. There is no point going through the motions of anything, especially prayer, if our heart isn't in it. Being ready means tending to our inner lives.

Saturday
Matthew 25:14–30

'... entrusted his property to them.'

The gospel today speaks to us about taking risks. We never discover how the first two servants managed to double their money in such a short time. One focus of the story is that the master trusted the servants, just as God trusts us with all the gifts of our minds and hearts. God asks us to use our true wealth to enrich the world: our capacity to love, to heal, to encourage and to spread joy. Sometimes that means taking a risk to reach out.

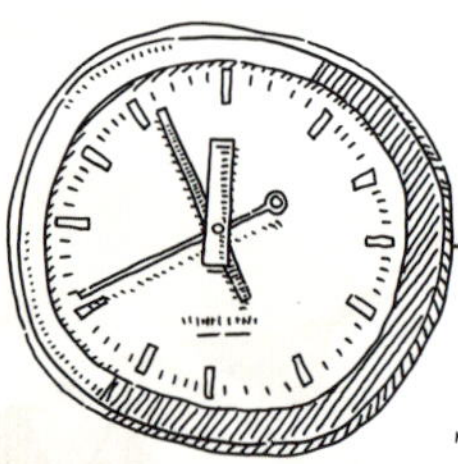

Week 22

This week, we begin travelling with Luke's Gospel. Have you ever thought about how important prayer is to Luke? Indeed, without Luke's Gospel the entire spirituality of Christianity would be quite different. We would not have the Hail Mary, the Magnificat, the *Nunc Dimittis* ('Now, Master, you can let your servant go in peace'), the *Benedictus* ('Blessed be the Lord') or even the *Gloria*. More than that, when Jesus is baptized, Luke, unlike Matthew and Mark, says that the Holy Spirit came on Jesus while he was 'at prayer'. The same thing happens at the transfiguration: unlike in the gospels of Matthew and Mark, Jesus is transfigured 'as he prayed'. Luke always wants to emphasize the close relationship Jesus had with his Father. There is a lot we can learn from Luke's warm-hearted spirituality. Prayer is at the heart of our reality, not an escape from it. It is openness to God, not trying to tell God what to do.

Prayer for Week 22

God of my prayer, The friend who sits with me, the friend who always turns up, the friend who never tires of listening, the friend who knows what I really meant to say, let me do something for you today, just for a change. Amen.

Monday
Luke 4:16–30

'... he has anointed me to bring the good news to the poor.'

Jesus has just returned from 40 days and nights in the desert. During that time, he had answered some tough questions about himself and what he valued. He had sorted himself out. His townsfolk were not so happy. They expected him to stick with a role assigned to him from birth. We are all called to keep growing, no matter what others may think.

Tuesday
Luke 4:31–37

'... he commands the unclean spirits ... '

Jesus made a deep impression because he spoke with authority. The world these days is full of image-makers and self-promoters. There are people who want to become rich and powerful by treating others like puppets. This was always the case. Jesus was different. He allowed people to discover their freedom.

Wednesday
Luke 4:38–44

'I must proclaim the good news of the kingdom of God ...'

Put yourself for a moment in the place of Simon's mother-in-law. Perhaps she was resigned to death. She may have been scared or unsure. Jesus gave her a new lease on life. He did the same for people who were brought to him by their friends. What would it have been like to have had this kind of encounter with Jesus? In which of our needs will he meet us today?

Thursday
Luke 5:1–11

'Put out into the deep water ...'

A good deal of Jesus' ministry took place near the water. Even after he rose from the dead, he met his disciples by the lake in Galilee (John 21). He wanted to return to where the adventure of faith had begun. We read about that beginning today. You would hardly have expected small business owners, steady folk used to working for themselves, to allow their lives to be overturned. But they did.

Friday
Luke 5:33–39

'... new wine must be put into fresh wineskins.'

Jesus clearly enjoyed life. He enjoyed a good meal with both friends and strangers, rich and poor. He also enjoyed a belief that life challenges our imaginations and asks us to be faithful and loving in creative ways. He loved both new wine and new wineskins. He didn't want to see any of us stuck in a comfortable groove.

Saturday
Luke 6:1–5

'The Son of Man is lord of the Sabbath.'

The greatest moments in life are when our frailty encounters God's strength, when our self-deception encounters God's vision. St. Paul says in a beautiful passage that 'the Spirit reaches the depths of everything, even the depths of God.' Our depths can only be known by the Holy Spirit. Jesus shows us this in today's gospel. The Pharisees are blinded by their shallow expectations of life's possibilities.

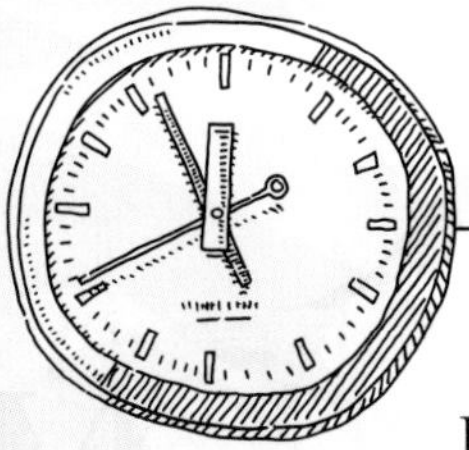

Week 23

In his book *Holy Living*, Rowan Williams, a former Archbishop of Canterbury, writes that 'to be fully human is to be recreated in the image of Christ's humanity'. This means 'a pouring out of life towards the Other'. These sentiments are very close to us in the gospel readings this week. Take a few moments to savour the words and phrases we find in Luke's Gospel as we journey in faith from day to day: to do good, to save life, happy are you, listening, compassionate, see clearly, good fruit, foundations on rock, tormented, trying to touch him. Now, try an old primary school exercise: put all these expressions into a single sentence. Please God, that sentence is our life.

Prayer for Week 23

God of my car, Can you do the driving this week? I need to rest in the passenger seat. Take me anywhere. Point out all the beauty along the way. Bring me home at the end of the day. Pick me up again in the morning. Amen.

HEADS UP
PHONES DOWN
City of
STONNINGTON
TOWARDS ZERO
VICTORIA POLICE

Monday
Luke 6:6–11

'... he knew what they were thinking ...'

The world is full of bystanders, people who sit back and wait for others to trip up so they can sit in judgment. The Pharisees were like this, trying to match reality to all the rules and regulations in their book. Christian life doesn't work like that. We are called to get into life, not sit on the sidelines. Jesus says to do good and save life. He doesn't mean just talking about those things.

Tuesday
Luke 6:12–19

'... he spent the night in prayer to God.'

Can we imagine our own names among the list of apostles we encounter today? How would Jesus approach us? What does he say to us this day to encourage us to join this group of intimate friends, with all the risks that involves? How does God win our heart?

Wednesday
Luke 6:20–26

'... leap for joy ...'

Happiness is an industry selling something that can't be bought. You hear people say, 'If only a certain thing happens, then I'll be happy.' A powerful word in Luke's beatitudes is *now*. Happy are you who weep *now*. Happy are you who are hungry *now*. Happiness is about the experience of hope in the present moment, not about loading up a credit card to pay off in the future.

Thursday
Luke 6:27–38

'Give, and it will be given for you ...'

We all know mean-spirited people and others who hold a grudge. We know people who pick fights with neighbours about things that hardly matter. We know colleagues who will never put someone else's cup in the dishwasher because it is 'not my job'. Jesus calls us to vibrant and even outrageous living. 'The measure you give will be the measure you get back.'

Friday
Luke 6:39–42

'Can a blind person guide a blind person?'

There are so many images of sight in the gospels. John's Gospel is especially famous for images of light and dark. Luke reminds us that we can all be blind, especially when we think we are somehow superior. Sometimes Jesus' background as a carpenter comes through. He surely knew what it meant to have a plank in the eye. He asks us to have a good hard look in the mirror and learn to love the person we see there with honesty and humility.

Saturday
Luke 6:43–49

'No good tree bears bad fruit ...'

Jesus drew many images from the natural world. Today he mentions not just grapes, figs, thorns and brambles but also floods and rock. He knew that creation had much to teach us and that we should try to develop a sensitive relationship with it. 'The good person out of the good treasure of the heart produces good ...' We are part of a bigger picture.

Week 24

The gospels all describe the special role of women in the life and work of Jesus. Luke's Gospel, however, has some unique stories; we come across several of them this week. Luke, for example, most helps us to get to know Mary, the mother of Jesus. There are other women characters whom you only find in Luke. They include Mary's relative Elizabeth, (chapter 1), Anna, an elderly wisdom figure (chapter 2), Martha and Mary (chapter 10), the crippled woman (chapter 13), the woman who loses a coin (chapter 15), the widow who petitions the judge (chapter 18), and the women of Jerusalem who weep as Jesus carries his cross (chapter 23).

In this week's gospel readings, we meet the widow of Nain (chapter 7) on Tuesday, the homeless woman at the house of Simon the Pharisee (chapter 7) on Thursday and the women who travel with Jesus (chapter 8) on Friday. Women are central to the way Luke tells the story. He has a respect for their strength, wisdom and leadership.

Prayer for Week 24

God of my kitchen, Thank you for the blessing of all the people with whom I have shared food. May I take time to reverence the blessings of food and drink and remember the lost, the lonely, the luckless and all those who live in fear. May we find in you a companion for all times and a lover of all people. Amen.

SURROUND YOURSELF WITH WOMEN WHO EMPOWER YOU
Fill this frame with a photo of the people that make you feel empowered every day.

Monday
Luke 7:1–10

'I am not worthy to have you come under my roof.'

We need this story these days. A Roman officer built a synagogue for the local people. In another time and place, he may have built a mosque as well. He is a man of authority in what was a truly brutal army. Yet, he has a tender heart and loves his daughter. It is his heart Jesus sees, not his uniform, not his sword.

Tuesday
Luke 7:11–17

'God has looked favourably on his people.'

A widow was a vulnerable figure in the world of Jesus. This woman had now lost her son, who was probably her only means of support. At the time of the funeral, there were many people offering her comfort. But what would the future hold? The hardest part of grief can be when the rest of the world has gone back to normal. Jesus responded from his heart. Can we do the same?

Wednesday
Luke 7:31–35

'We played the flute for you, and you did not dance ...'

Jesus had clearly been listening to the children singing in the marketplace. He remembered one of their songs, which is all about people who miss the moment because they can only see and act in conventional ways. Jesus asks us to be fully alive in the present moment, sensitive to the new things God is doing. That means today.

Thursday
Luke 7:36–50

'Which of them will love him more?'

This chapter of Luke's Gospel is full of tenderness. The woman at the house of Simon the Pharisee is a beautiful example. The ointment she rubbed into Jesus' feet was sensual. Even more so was the way she used her hair to wipe the feet of Jesus. Simon was clearly threatened by such a display. Jesus wasn't. He is never threatened by anyone.

Friday
Luke 8:1–3

'... provided for them out of their resources.'

We'd love to know more about the women who travelled with Jesus, sharing the same position as 'the twelve'. Indeed, the line that these women 'provided for them out of their resources' suggests they had some money – a rarity in Jesus' culture, as was their ability to travel 'through cities and villages'. They are not easy to fit into regular categories. Jesus made them welcome. He didn't think in social stereotypes.

Saturday
Luke 8:4–15

'... an honest and good heart ...'

Jesus compared the word of God to a seed. It is a wonderful image because a seed is not the plant or tree, only the place that the plant or tree begins. When we encounter the word of God, it is not complete, as some people would have us believe. It needs to find rich soil, meaning people with 'an honest and good heart'. May we all find such a heart in ourselves and allow the seed to grow.

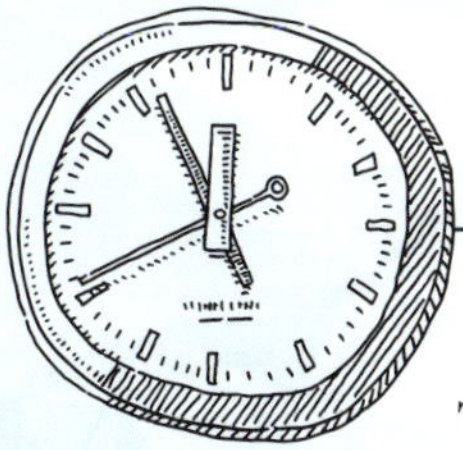

Week 25

This is the time of year when seasons change most dramatically. The hours of daylight lengthen or shorten, depending on where you are, most rapidly. In many ways, the Christian story travels close to the cycles of nature. Simone Weil (1909–1943), whose difficult journey led her to become a great spiritual philosopher, said that the whole world was like a white stick in the hands of blind people. It is there to help us find our way towards the God we cannot see, but whose reality is all around us. This week, the gospel readings from St. Luke engage with the world in dramatic, creative and risky ways. We are all called to do the same.

Prayer for Week 25

God of changing seasons, Open our hearts to the wonder of the world. Make us sensitive to the signs of your grace at work, in both beauty and disfigurement, light and dark, colour and greyness, good days and not-so-good days. May we be people of hope, rather than fake sentiment and timid attachment. Amen.

Monday
Luke 8:16–18

'... nor is anything secret that will not become known and come to light.'

There are plenty of people who make it difficult to get close to them. They often have complex reasons for presenting an image to the world. Maybe they need to be seen as competent, authoritative or in control. Others like to be seen as the opposite, hiding their abilities and allowing others to take the risks. When Jesus asks us to put our light in plain view, he is reminding us that our true selves have more to offer others than any pretence.

Tuesday
Luke 8:19–21

'... those who hear the word of God and do it.'

When Jesus kept his mother and brothers waiting outside, he may not have been as rude as he appears. He was simply saying that his family is very large and open to all who are serious about their faith. His words conveyed a welcome, not hostility. Please God, this day our lives will embrace those who cross our paths.

Wednesday
Luke 9:1–6

'Take nothing for your journey ...'

Have you ever been on a plane and wondered about the person who arrives with no luggage? Their journey seems easier, less cluttered and freer. Jesus asks us to board the plane with nothing but the clothes we stand up in. He doesn't believe in paying for excess baggage. He wants us to have space for the experiences yet to come.

Thursday
Luke 9:7–9

'Who is this about whom I hear such things?'

Herod's whole life was one of confusion and anxiety. Killing John the Baptist did not solve any of his problems. It only made more. You can hear the fear in his voice. 'Who is this about whom I hear such things?' The text says he wanted to see Jesus. It does not say he wanted to meet him or encounter him or listen to him or converse. Such a pity. Fear destroys. Encounter heals. Fear only has a past. Encounter has a present and a future.

Friday
Luke 9:18–22

'The Son of Man must undergo great suffering ...'

Jesus calls us to an authentic personal relationship. He first asked who the crowds said he was. That question was easy. He then asked, 'Who do you say that I am?' That was a much harder one. Peter was a leader because he was prepared to take the leap of faith that saw further and deeper than the mob.

Saturday
Luke 9:43–45

'... it was concealed from them.'

Today's gospel presents one of those moments when Jesus is the flavour of the month. He was, as we say these days, riding high in the opinion polls: '... everyone was amazed at all that he was doing.' It was part of his clear-sighted sense of mission that he knew this wouldn't last long. He could see past the hype to his true purpose. His friends didn't understand and were afraid to ask questions that may have had dangerous answers.

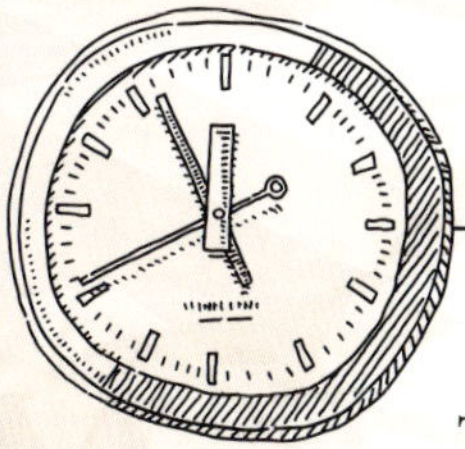

Week 26

The Danish writer Isak Dinesen (1882–1965) lived in many places. Her time in Kenya, for example, led to the book *Out of Africa*, which was made into a movie. She is remembered as saying that 'the Earth was made round so that we would not see too far down the road.' Of course, she was speaking figuratively, but she made a good point. It is similar to the thought attributed to the Chinese philosopher Confucius: 'Roads were made for journeys, not destinations.' Once again, the gospel readings this week are full of stories from 'on the road'. The Greek word for road, *oder*, gives us the word 'synodality', which means a road taken together or a shared journey. Life is the name we give to the journey God shares with us.

Prayer for Week 26

God of laughter, We thank you for the fun in our lives and also for the joy. Joy lasts longer and may go deeper. Fun is today; joy is a lifestyle. Fun is still good, an experience of grace, a rung on the ladder to joy and to you, who tickles our ribs, forever and ever. Amen.

CREST
SLOW DOWN

Monday
Luke 9:46–50

'… whoever is not against you is for you.'

Around this time of year, we celebrate a few feasts for angels. There have been people in my life whom I think of as guardian angels. I can't forget their kindness and gentleness. When we read in Scripture that the angels are always in the presence of God, we realize that such gracious acts do bring us all closer to God, the source of all love.

Tuesday
Luke 9:51–56

'… they did not receive him, because his face was set toward Jerusalem.'

The Samaritans were suspicious of Jerusalem and prejudiced against Jesus' friends because they were headed in that direction. We might think the same of people because they come from or are headed to anyplace in the world, even a suburb or town a few miles away. If someone told us they were heading off to Tehran or Pyongyang or Tripoli or some other place that makes us a bit nervous, would we reject them? Jesus believes that moving on is better than carrying the burden of antagonism.

Wednesday
Luke 9:57–62

'… no one who … looks back is fit for the kingdom.'

For Jesus, the road is home. 'The heart does not rest until it rests in God,' as St. Augustine famously said. Burying one's parents is a sacred trust, and there are many stories in which Jesus is compassionate to those in grief. Yet, he doesn't want us to be stuck in nostalgia, regrets or remorse. Hope is a compass, not a pillow.

Thursday
Luke 10:1–12

'… the harvest is plentiful, but the labourers are few.'

Jesus had the same message for both those who welcomed his friends and those who rejected them: 'The kingdom of God has come near to you.' Our blindness or unkindness can't stop grace working in the world. Yet, the decisions we make can help God's love find a home on the road. Wherever we go, said Jesus, our first words should be 'Peace be with you.' We can bring positive energy to every situation, just as God does.

Friday
Luke 10:13–16

'Whoever listens to you listens to me …'

The most hard-and-fast instruction in *The Rule of St Benedict,* a wise and beautiful guide for people striving to find God in community, is the very first word: listen. 'Listen carefully, my child, my instructions and attend to them with the ear of your heart. This is advice from one who loves you.' Listening is a rare skill. We warm to those friends who take time to understand what we are trying to say. Jesus said, 'Anyone who listens to you listens to me.' If we want people to listen to us, we must know what listening means in the first place.

Saturday
Luke 10:17–24

'Blessed are the eyes that see what you see!'

The scene of Jesus' friends returning to him with stories from the road is delightful. They were like children returning from a day at school or a camp, excited by what they had learned and achieved. Jesus was so happy for them. They were starting to understand. They had experienced the liberating power of his message. He hopes we might share the same kind of childlike exhilaration.

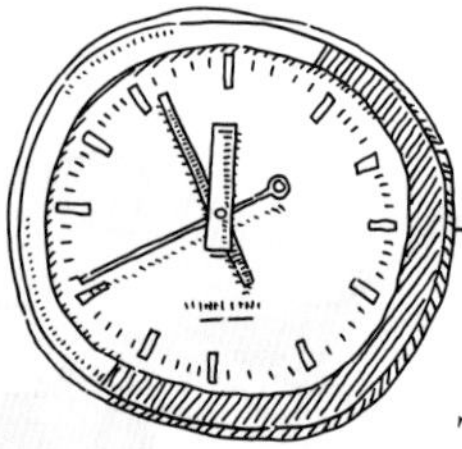

Week 27

The older we get, the harder we find it to jump. We look at children tumbling around and perhaps feel a little nostalgic for the time when our bones could do the same thing. This also applies to what many people have called 'the leap of faith'. Perhaps we can recall a time when we knew, deep in our being, that God was real and that we were loved and understood, regardless of all our painful shortcomings. We took our first leap of faith, trusting that God would catch us and hold us. We were not to realize how often God would ask us to jump, to spring up and leap into the unknown. God asks this of us over and over again. No matter how much older we grow, our spirits can soar, appreciating the beauty of life, leaving its frustrations on the ground.

Prayer for Week 27

God of our seeking, May we find you in our reality, enjoying the signs you leave for us in every tree, every meal, every friend, every longing, every need, every happiness, every confusion. Help us to put the clues together, to find you waiting, who is forever patient and playful. Amen.

JUMP

Monday
Luke 10:25–37

'And who is my neighbour?'

How many times have we heard the story of the Good Samaritan? It is easy to understand but far more challenging to put into practice. In *Fratelli Tutti* (2020), Pope Francis wrote about this parable:

> We need to acknowledge that we are constantly tempted to ignore others, especially the weak. Let us admit that, for all the progress we have made, we are still "illiterate" when it comes to accompanying, caring for and supporting the most frail and vulnerable members of our developed societies. We have become accustomed to looking the other way, passing by, ignoring situations until they affect us directly. (para 64)

Tuesday
Luke 10:38–42

'Lord, do you not care?'

It is easy to forget that Martha and Mary were sisters, given their different approaches to life. There are times for stillness and times for action. In the story of Lazarus (John 11:1–43), their roles are flipped, at least initially. Martha is the one who goes out to welcome Jesus. She challenges him while Mary remains at home. The Martha part of us and the Mary part of us need to love each other and keep each other in balance.

Wednesday
Luke 11:1–4

'... give us each day our daily bread.'

The Lord's Prayer embraces an entire spirituality in just a few lines: surrender, longing, gratitude, forgiveness and openness. Let us take time to allow every line to resonate with our experience of today.

Thursday
Luke 11:5–13

'... everyone who searches finds ...'

What are we searching for today? Whose door are we knocking on in our longing for a deeper faith? Do we trust that God will give us bread and not a stone? Fish and not a snake? Jesus said, 'Ask'. He wants to hear our questions. He wants us to trust his response to our neediness.

Friday
Luke 11:15–26

'Every kingdom divided against itself becomes a desert ...'

The devil doesn't wear horns and a cape. The enemy of human nature is clothed in cynicism, opportunism, indifference, callousness, harshness, point scoring and inflexibility. God's grace is stronger than any of this. Love is strong. It stands guard against our fall from grace.

Saturday
Luke 11:27–28

'Blessed are those who hear the word of God and obey it!'

Jesus often spoke about happiness. He said, 'Blessed are those who hear the word of God and obey it'. In some small way, we will hear the word of God today. Keeping that word surely means attending to the way we live, responding in gratitude to the gift of every experience. But keeping has another meaning. It means holding onto something and protecting it. In a throwaway world, the word of God is not disposable.

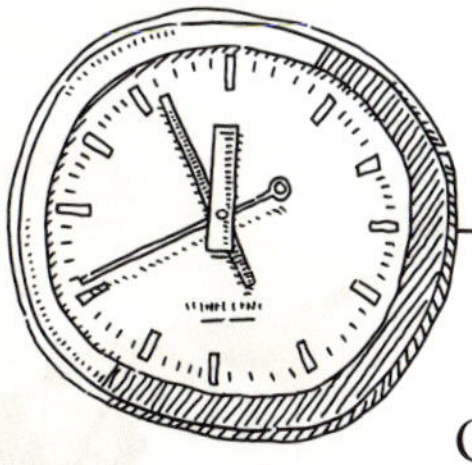

Week 28

October is often a month that brings a mild sense of panic. There are so many things that need to be done before the end of the calendar year. Christmas is suddenly looming on the horizon, and we may begin making lists of what we need to achieve in the next couple of months. Can we recall our last new year's resolution? It may be a distant memory now that we are in the thick of life's demands. This is the time of year when Catholics focus on the Rosary, that most calming and gentle form of prayer that brings stillness and focus to a frenetic day. This week's readings from the Gospel of Luke all share a common question. They ask over and over what is important in our lives. These are the central chapters of the gospel where priorities get sorted out. They call us to change from caterpillars into butterflies and to learn how to fly.

Prayer for Week 28

God of my backpack, my shopping bag, my computer case, my gym bag, my on-board luggage, make me aware of the burdens I carry and those I make for others. Help me to travel more lightly. I need nothing more than I need you, my companion and guide, today and forever. Amen.

I had time to be much amused. 1873
Mary MacKillop
1842 – 1909
www.sosj.org.au

Monday
Luke 11:29–32

'... something greater than Jonah is here!'

People ask Jesus for a sign. Perhaps they should ask for *another* sign. They are already surrounded by countless signs of God's love and purpose. The story of Jonah to which Jesus referred is full of irony and humour, hallmarks of the way God communicates with us. Our lives are like rooms in a detective story. God's fingerprints are everywhere. We need to stop moving and attend to God's subtle ways.

Tuesday
Luke 11:37–41

'... inside you are full of greed and wickedness.'

We'd love to be in the room when Jesus came to eat with the Pharisee, a person whose name we don't even know. The Pharisee is clearly open-minded, and his surprise about Jesus not washing may be just as much about the comfort and hygiene of his guest as about observing a ritual. Jesus is not interested in social niceties. He wants our hearts.

Wednesday
Luke 11:42–46

'... you ... neglect justice and the love of God.'

Jesus had a go at lawyers for making burdens and laying them on the shoulders of people. We do this to others, and we do it to ourselves. Jesus wants us to give ourselves a break, not to sweat the small stuff so much, such as tithing on mint and rue. His language was strong. We get so caught up in things that don't matter that we become the living dead, 'like unmarked graves'. Jesus calls us to life.

Thursday
Luke 11:47–54

'... taken away the key of knowledge!'

Jesus mourned the human history of bloodshed that extended from Abel to Zechariah, from A to Z. Sadly, that history is far from over. There is so much conflict and violence in the world that it is tempting to turn away. Who can cope? Part of what Jesus said is that we must cope with being unable to cope. Peace is only possible if we can embrace the pain of others.

Friday
Luke 12:1–7

'Are not five sparrows sold for two pennies?'

Go into the garden or a park. Find a small stone. Hold it for a minute. That stone is millions of years old. It has witnessed the whole of history. Yet, it has no monetary value at all. 'Are not five sparrows sold for two pennies?' asked Jesus. A glass of water from our tap at home costs less than a cent. There is a world of difference between value and price. Value is the inherent, often hidden worth of things.

Saturday
Luke 12:9–12

'... the Holy Spirit will teach you ... what you ought to say.'

There are plenty of guidebooks available for negotiating difficult conversations. There can be good sense in this, thinking through the best way to get a message across. Jesus said not to worry about what to say: ' ... the Holy Spirit will teach you at that very hour what you ought to say.' We can relate to this as well. Even if we prepare for a difficult encounter, often enough we find a different path when we are face to face with a person. We become more empathetic. More aware of both their pain and our own. We find words that give life.

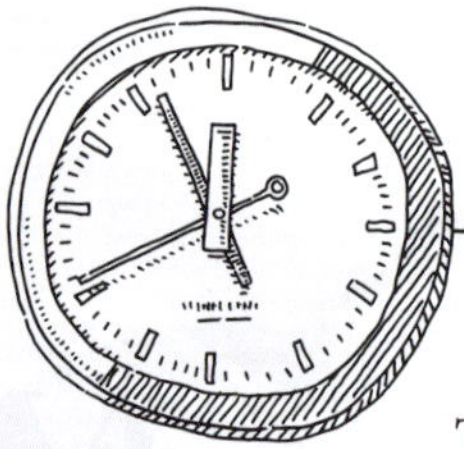

Week 29

The gospel readings this week offer many thoughts about preparing for the future. They tell us to be ready for nerve-racking events we can't predict. There is a sense here that some grim times lie in wait for us. How do we deal with this? Christians often distinguish between optimism and hope. Optimism can be like putting your head in the sand, blithely expecting everything will turn out for the best. Hope is a much deeper openness to reality and to grace. Optimism is more passive; hope rolls up its sleeves. Optimism thinks it won't get burned in the sun; hope puts on a hat and sunscreen. Jesus calls us to be people of hope. For us, forever is a place of the heart.

Prayer for Week 29

God of the nightly news, We offer to you the endless parade of the world's suffering and anxiety. Bring peace to every place, compassion to every heart, hope to every mind, openness to every hand. May we beat swords into ploughshares and let anger evaporate from the earth, starting with ourselves. Amen.

Monday
Luke 12:13–21

'... life does not consist in ... possessions ...'

Jesus was not impressed by people who stored up treasure for themselves. Elsewhere, he said that 'where your treasure is, there your heart will be also.' What do we really value? Jesus knows that our life can't be made secure by anything we own. There is another kind of security that comes from deep faith in God and surrender to a mystery we can never possess for ourselves. St. Paul says only three things last: faith, hope and love. The greatest of these is love. It is also the most challenging.

Tuesday
Luke 12:35–38

'... have your lamps lit.'

Happy is sometimes translated as *blessed*. Happy are the servants who open the door when the Lord comes at an awkward hour. For us, this might be when a distressed friend calls just as we have sat down. Or when a child needs to be picked up late and we have an early start the next day. These are the times when the Lord is really waiting on us. It takes faith to see that they are times of blessing, of happiness. The gift we receive is called inconvenience, a pebble in our shoe that reminds us that God is the boss.

Wednesday
Luke 12:39–48

'... even more will be demanded.'

Simple faithfulness is not as widely appreciated as it could be. There is as much inspiration in an elderly couple who care for each other, day in and day out, as there is in a young sports star who breaks a record. A paramedic who waits for hours on a hospital ramp with a patient is never going to make headlines. But these people are truly awake. They are faithful to God's unexpected arrival.

Thursday
Luke 12:49–53

'I came to bring fire to the earth ...'

In a charming movie called *The Best Exotic Marigold Hotel* (2011), one of the characters says that everything will be all right in the end. If things are not all right, it just means it is not yet the end. When Jesus talked about a fire coming to the earth and about so much division, he was not saying that these things are ideal. They are the reality we are called to work with and pray within. We help carry our communities through and beyond them.

Friday
Luke 12:54–59

'Why do you not judge ... what is upright?'

Jesus asked, 'Why do you not know how to interpret the present time?' He made it sound easy. It's not. How can we make sense of the many problems facing the human family without simplifying them or reducing them to slogans? How can we face our troubled reality without building fences between us and other people? Interpreting the times means accepting that God is at work in every heart, every mind, every longing, every dream. That is the place to start. If we can't understand someone, we can remind ourselves that at least God understands them.

Saturday
Luke 13:1–9

'... until I dig around it and put manure on it.'

We don't know much about the 18 people who died when a tower fell on them at Siloam, an area in the southern part of Jerusalem. Jesus made the point that people who suffer calamities are no worse or better than the rest of us. In fact, they are just like us. Repentance means change. How can we change to become more compassionate?

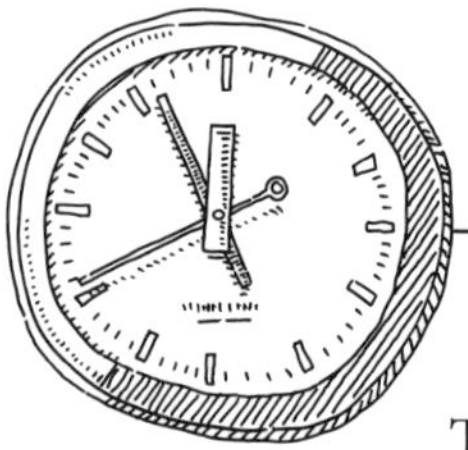

Week 30

There is nowhere any of us can pray other than the present moment. God meets us faithfully in our reality. As we grow in faith, we sometimes realize that God is more comfortable with our reality than we are. We all have memories that make us feel embarrassed or even ashamed; other memories may make us feel angry or afraid. They may not be comfortable. We also have dreams for the future. Hopes, plans, ambitions, goals. God is fine with all who we happen to be. But right now, this day, God calls us to fully inhabit our own lives and to find intimacy with God in the here and now. This week's gospel stories are full of here-and-now moments: an argument about the Sabbath, a tour of towns and villages, anger about Herod, a meal with an educated person. Our week will also be full of happenings and events. God is waiting in them for us.

Prayer for Week 30

God of quiet days, May we find you in stillness, in the sound of the birds outside, in a gentle knock on our door. Help us notice your presence in the sounds far off, the subtle tastes, the delicate smells, the gentle touches. May all our senses be open to you. Amen.

WE MAKE
POSSIBLE

Monday
Luke 13:10–17

'…the entire crowd was rejoicing…'

The Sabbath was and is a beautiful custom. It's a pity we don't observe it more. We all need some quiet time and time with family. Society has swung from one extreme to the other. Instead of hearing 'How dare you break the Sabbath?' we are more likely to hear, 'How dare you keep the Sabbath?' or perhaps 'How can you manage to take time off?' But even a good thing is not an absolute. Surely helping a woman who has been bent over for 18 years is more important. Justice and compassion are the signs of a living faith.

Tuesday
Luke 13:18–21

'What is the kingdom of God like?'

We often think of the mustard seed and fail to notice the idea that the kingdom of God is a place with branches in which the birds of the air can find shelter. It is a beautiful image. When we pray every day 'your kingdom come', we are praying for safety and security for all God's creatures, especially the most vulnerable. Where will our hearts find shelter today?

Wednesday
Luke 13:22–30

'…some are last who will be first.'

The word 'door' occurs dozens of times in the New Testament. Obviously, a door is a useful and familiar object, and Scripture is full of those: shoes, plates, cups and plenty of others. A door is also a great image of opening our hearts and lives to God. Jesus asks us to knock. And keep knocking. And still more to keep knocking.

Thursday
Luke 13:31–35

'…I must be on my way…'

Jesus called Herod a 'fox'. It was one of the harshest things he ever said about anyone, and the insult was well deserved. By contrast, using a feminine image, Jesus compared himself to a hen gathering her chicks under her wings. Foxes love making raids on chickens. The metaphor surely applies these days to the behaviour of manipulative and exploitative people. We are all vulnerable to those. God, as the psalms remind us, is our strength and our shield.

Friday
Luke 14:1–6

'…they were watching him closely.'

'And they could not reply to this.' The same thing goes for us. God challenges us and surprises us in many ways. God gets us to think again even about things we hold dear, the equivalent for us of the Sabbath. God leaves us speechless.

Saturday
Luke 14:7–11

'Do not sit down at the place of honour.'

When I was at school, the place of honour on the bus was at the back, not the front. That's where the cool kids sat. The same applied at the movies. Often enough, people like to sit at the back of church, and it's hard to get them to sit closer to the front. Never mind. Jesus' message is still the same. We are called to sit with the lonely, the awkward and the difficult. Not with the 'in' crowd. 'For all who exalt themselves will be humbled, and those who humble themselves will be exalted.'

Week 31

This is the time of year when we think in a special way of people who have died, including those who have been part of our lives and whom we have loved. Sometimes our memories are tinged with sorrow, especially if a death is recent or a loss is deeply painful. We wonder what God might have had in mind. Perhaps it is better to think of God as a companion on difficult days more than as the one who comes up with answers. On other occasions, we experience deep gratitude for people who have shaped us and shown us the path to life. Perhaps this week and next we can give a few minutes of our prayer time each day simply to remember a different person who has helped us grow into the person we have become.

Prayer for Week 31

God of the living, We thank you for all the people you have brought into our lives, especially those who have died. May we know that they are praying for us as we relish their memory with love and gratitude, and even joy. They have brought your grace to us and continue to do so. Amen.

Monday
Luke 14:12–14

'... do not invite your friends or your brothers or your relatives or rich neighbours ...'

Jesus asks us to make a special place for 'the poor, the crippled, the lame, and the blind'. It doesn't matter that they cannot pay you back. In the language of today, Jesus was speaking out against what we call 'transactional relationships'. These are pragmatic relationships that function a bit like 'you scratch my back and I'll scratch yours'. We are called to love people for who they are, not what they are, and even less for what they can do for us.

Tuesday
Luke 14:15–24

'Go out at once into the streets and lanes ...'

For two days in a row, the gospel has spoken of making room for 'the poor, the crippled, the blind, and the lame'. The master said to make sure that 'my house may be filled'. Jesus is only too aware that those who are doing well in life get caught up in their worries about real estate, property and even romance. Jesus asks us always to keep a wider perspective. God's concerns are broader than ours.

Wednesday
Luke 14:25–33

'... if you do not give up all your possessions.'

Not many of us have set out to build a tower. But most of us have tried at some stage to build a career or a ministry or a family or a community. Jesus seemed to say that the cost of creating something important may well be greater than we first thought. Are we prepared to put ourselves and our egos on the line? 'Whoever does not carry the cross and follow me cannot be my disciple.'

Thursday
Luke 15:1–10

'... there is joy in the presence of the angels of God ...'

The image of God as a seeker is powerful. Like a shepherd who has lost a sheep or a woman who has lost a coin, God turns everything upside down until our hearts are found. Even this day, something irritating or disturbing may simply be God at work, trying to find us in some corner of our lives where we are lost.

Friday
Luke 16:1–8

'... the children of this age are more shrewd ...'

Jesus seemed to praise the dishonest steward in the parable. Perhaps the worker's skill is being able to deal with the reality of his situation and craft a solution that works to his advantage. These days, his actions would land him in jail. The message is that we must live in the demands of our lives and be astute, wise and discerning.

Saturday
Luke 16:9–15

'God knows your hearts.'

Jesus knew a lot about money. Thirty pieces of silver, 100 denarii, the head of Caesar on a coin, the widow's mite, the workers who came late, the parable of the talents, the gold at his birth, the traders in the temple, the tax collector, the treasure in a field, the pearl of great price, the lots cast for his underwear, the rich young man who went away sad, the eye of a needle. Today we read, 'Make friends ... by means of dishonest wealth.' Jesus built deep questions around such stories and images. What are we making of the world? Why? How will we grow?

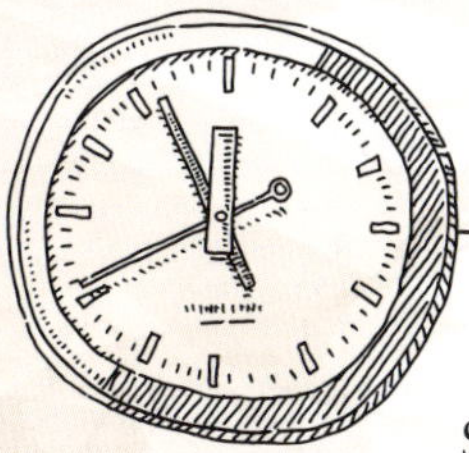

Week 32

Some people like to carve their names into church pews. Apart from being vandalism, it is unnecessary. God knows all our names. In the book of the Prophet Isaiah, we are told that we are carved on the palm of God's hands. The image reminds me of all the things we may have written on our hands or wrists so we don't forget them: a phone number or an address or some important fact. They soon wash off. God never washes us off. This is reassuring because there is a sense in the gospel readings this week that life is precarious. Even our faith can be a delicate balance. The more threatening the world becomes, the more deeply we need to cling to the basics. Our lives are the way God is engraved on the world.

Prayer for Week 32

God of my empty bowl, Replace my hungers with hunger only for you. Fill my hours with peace, my days with hope, my weeks with love, my years with faith, for you alone feed us forever and ever. Amen.

Monday

Luke 17:1–6

'... if you had faith the size of a mustard seed ...'

Jesus offers three succinct messages.
1. Obstacles are sure to come.
2. Forgiveness is not an optional extra.
3. Even a small faith can work wonders.
To each of these messages, we can only respond in gratitude.

Tuesday

Luke 17:7–10

'We are worthless slaves ...'

Sometimes you hear people say that they like giving to causes or volunteering their time because 'it makes me feel good.' That is all well and good, but living justly is inherent to our growth as human beings. It is in our nature to be generous. This is the meaning of duty: it is something we can hardly choose not to do. Jesus asks us to remind ourselves that 'we have done only what we ought to have done.' St. Augustine said that 'in doing what we ought, we deserve no praise, because it is our duty.'

Wednesday

Luke 17:11–19

'Was none of them found to return and give praise to God except this foreigner?'

Sometimes teachers get cards of gratitude from people they helped years ago. This applies in other walks of life as well. Only a few people say thank you in a deep and thoughtful way. They make all the difference. Gratitude is a gift we give both ourselves and others. It reflects a truth that we have more done for us than we could ever do for ourselves.

Thursday

Luke 17:20–25

'... the kingdom of God is among you.'

The *Tao Te Ching*, the *Book of the Way*, an ancient Chinese text of spiritual guidance, contains some memorable lines: 'Fill your bowl to the brim and it will spill. Chase after money and security and your heart will never unclench. Care about people's approval and you will be their prisoner. Do your work, then step back.' When Jesus says, 'the kingdom of God is among you', he reminds us that it is not in the usual places we look.

Friday

Luke 17:26–37

'Those who try to make their life secure will lose it ...'

Anybody who has held the hand of someone they loved as they passed from this life to the next knows that something extraordinary happens in that moment. There is surely an experience of grief and loss but also, often enough, a sense that a new phase of life is beginning. We let go of one reality and allow another to embrace us. God is endlessly creative, always making something happen, even with pain. It is an experience beyond words that ripples 'through the whole earth.'

Saturday

Luke 18:1–8

'... a widow who kept on coming to him ...'

Jesus invites us to pray continually and never lose heart. The poet George Herbert (1593–1633) described prayer as a banquet, the breath in our lungs, the soul in paraphrase, the heart in pilgrimage, a kind of tune, the land of spices. One of his images for prayer, that it is 'something understood', is exquisite. That understanding can take a long time. So, we stick with it, turning up every day to be consciously with the God who is never unconscious of us.

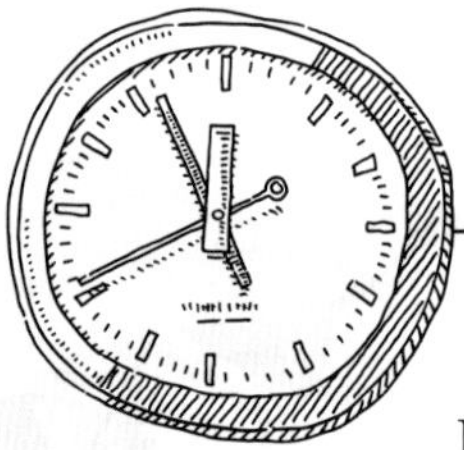

Week 33

Putting a house on the market is a nerve-racking time for both buyers and sellers. Many people who long for their own home may have the sinking feeling that they may never be able to afford even a modest place. The quest for a place to call home is very deep within us. It means security and belonging. That is why we feel so deeply for the millions of refugees in the world who flee their homes for fear of their lives. As the Christian year draws to a close, the theme of homecoming is in our hearts. Where has this year brought us? Where have we landed? What has changed in our lives since last Christmas? Where has the Lord made a home with us?

Prayer for Week 33

God of trees and ladders, Bring us back down to earth to walk beside you. May we encounter all life as part of your mystery as we make peace on earth. Amen.

HOMELESS
PLEASE
HELP

Monday
Luke 18:35–43

'... he shouted even more loudly ...'

Nobody can pretend to be blind. But we can close our eyes for a few moments and hear Jesus say those words to us: 'What do you want me to do for you?' The question is totally open to our reality, whatever it happens to be. What do we truly want God to do in our lives? Perhaps we might answer, 'Let me see again.' In other words, let me be more understanding, more aware, more compassionate.

Tuesday
Luke 19:1–10

'... I must stay at your house today.'

Jesus told Zacchaeus to get down from his tree. He says the same to us. We all climb trees to get a better position, one that is above others in some way. Jesus brings us back down to earth. He wants our feet on the ground. He wants to find us in our hiding places, bring us out into the open and sit down to eat with us.

Wednesday
Luke 19:11–28

'... they supposed that the kingdom of God was to appear immediately ...'

Jesus was disappointed in the servant who played it safe and would not take a chance. Sure, he held onto his one pound or gold coin. But that is not what it means to live a life in faith. On the contrary, it means to be adventurous, daring, alive to all of life's possibilities. This parable is not about making money. It is about living the biggest life of which we are capable.

Thursday
Luke 19:41–44

'... you did not recognize the time ...'

Jesus cried when he saw Jerusalem. This was his homeland, the city that meant so much to his culture and in the faith life of his people. He lamented, 'If you ... had only recognized on this day the things that make for peace'. We might say the same thing today, and might apply those words to ourselves. If only we understood how much we are called to work for peace.

Friday
Luke 19:45–48

'My house shall be a house of prayer ...'

Today's gospel tells us that Jesus' enemies were afraid of him 'for all the people were spellbound by what they heard.' Everyday people could appreciate his wisdom. Those who had positions of authority to defend could not. There is a timeless message here. A so-called leading citizen is not necessarily a wise one. Wisdom is more likely to be a grassroots experience. Those who understood the hard side of life knew that Jesus' words of faith and justice could create a far more humane future for everyone.

Saturday
Luke 20:27–40

'They no longer dared to ask him another question.'

My elderly aunt thought that any woman who had seven husbands deserved to go to heaven. She believed the answer to the question 'Whose wife will the woman be?' was 'None of them! She would have learned from her experience and given them all a wide berth.' At least my aunt saw the woman in the story as a real person. The Sadducees were playing intellectual games. Jesus tells them that God is God 'not of the dead, but of the living'.

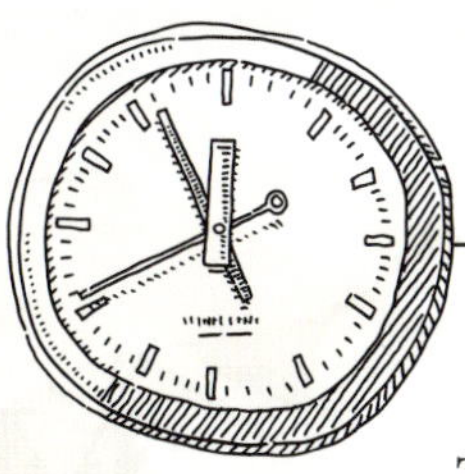

Week 34

This week is the last one in Ordinary Time and in the Church's year. Next Sunday we begin again, preparing for Christmas and, after that, embarking on Lent and the Easter Season, allowing ourselves to be caught up once more in the cycle of God's love. The liturgical seasons remind us of the different ways we encounter the Lord in all the times and places of our lives. This week's gospel readings are not always the most cheerful, speaking as they do of the end time when we should pray for 'strength to escape all these things that will take place'. Yet, they do offer a springboard into the hope we celebrate in Advent. Perhaps this week we can think of all the reasons we have to be grateful since this time last year. It's the time of year when shops carry little thank-you gifts that people give to teachers and work colleagues. What thank-you gift could we give to God? What words would we write on a card if we could send one to God?

Prayer for the last week of the Church year

God of all time, We thank you for this year, with all its hope and all its confusion. We thank you for the gift of our humanity. We are creatures and part of all creation. May the cycle of seasons and years remind us that we play a small part, but that we are loved, just as we are, forever and ever. Amen.

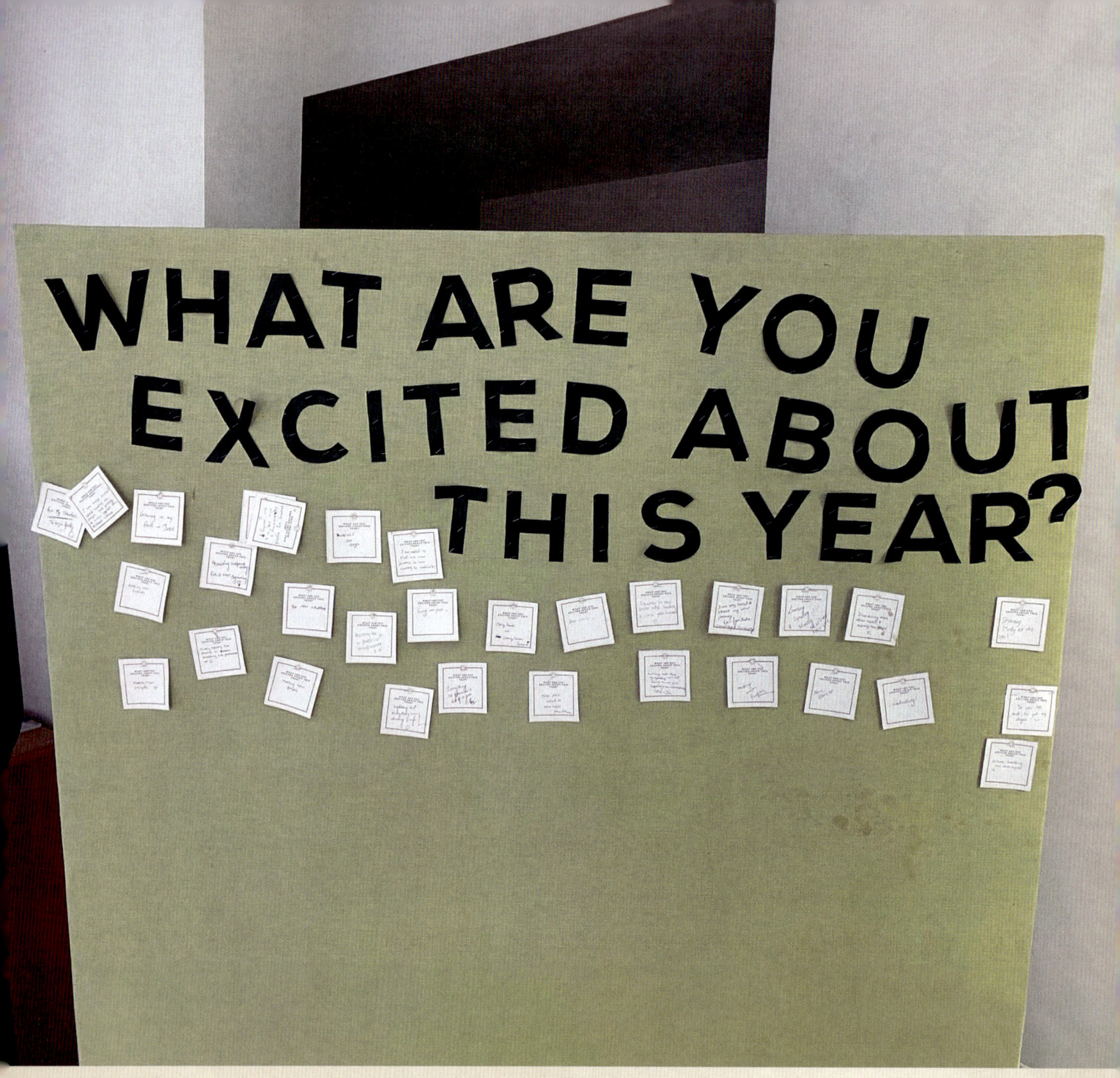
WHAT ARE YOU EXCITED ABOUT THIS YEAR?

Monday
Luke 21:1–4

'... this poor widow has put in more than all of them ...'

A friend of mine went to Jerusalem and bought two small coins from the time of Jesus, the same as those the woman had in today's iconic story. My friend paid a king's ransom for them because 'that widow has always meant so much to me'. I was confused. The story is about giving, not buying. The widow becomes a model for Jesus, who, like her, is soon to give all he has.

Tuesday
Luke 21:5–11

'... not one stone will be left on another ...'

The Letter to the Hebrews (13:14) says, 'For here we have no lasting city, but we are looking for the city that is to come.' Jesus seemed resigned to a future that would include many wars and much turmoil. No matter what happens, humans will tend to destructiveness. Besides that, people suffer through fires, floods and earthquakes. What do we have when so much has been destroyed? St. Paul writes that only three things truly last: faith, hope and love. 'The greatest of these is love.'

Wednesday
Luke 21:12–19

'I will give you words and a wisdom.'

Society at large has always been suspicious of authentic Christianity, and that tendency has certainly not improved in recent times. Most of us have known persecution, even if it is an offhand and dismissive remark. Jesus reminds us that there are times when we need to be thick skinned. We are in God's hands. 'I will give you words and a wisdom that none of your opponents will be able to withstand or contradict.'

Thursday
Luke 21:20–28

'There will be signs ...'

Jesus uses the world 'desolate'. St. Ignatius of Loyola described the inner movement of desolation as 'any decrease of faith, hope and love'. Most of us are familiar with it. Ignatius said to be patient, as we will soon be consoled. 'In desolation, make no change.' Jesus says, 'Hold your heads high, because your liberation is near at hand.'

Friday
Luke 21:29–33

'When you see these things taking place ...'

Today's gospel hits the perfect note for the end of the Christian year. It speaks of discernment, of reading the world around us in order to find our place in it. 'As soon as they sprout leaves you can see for yourselves and know that summer is already near.' In other words, look for the small signs of God's big dreams for us. 'Know that the kingdom of God is near.'

Saturday
Luke 21:34–36

'... stand before the Son of Man.'

Jesus says, 'Be alert at all times, praying that you may have the strength to escape all these things that will take place.' He warns us against escapism and urges us to hold our ground. In other words, to embrace all that life throws at us. Every moment is full to the brim with God's presence. No day is ordinary.

Also by Michael McGirr

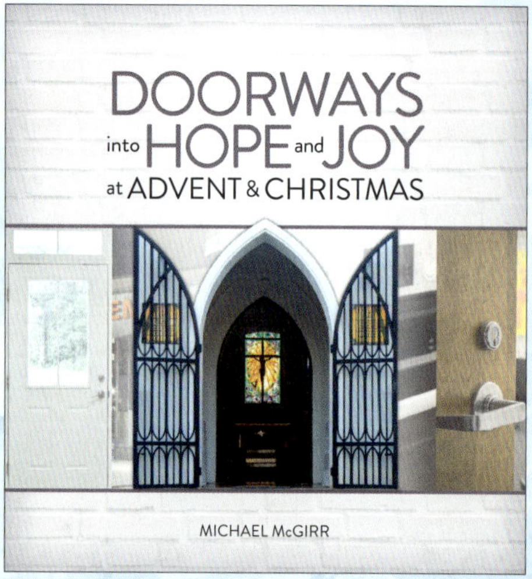

It's that time of year ...

Advent and Christmas are supposed to be seasons of quiet anticipation and peaceful wonder. Yet, despite what the carol says, we have few silent nights and even fewer days when all is calm. Advent and Christmas have become times laden with every kind of expectation: work parties, school holidays, present buying, heavy traffic, people to remember, and so on and so on.

These prayers are a little breather. A rest from the hype. A chance to just be ourselves for a moment, just as we are, with the God who wants to keep things simple. Hopefully these words and images can help turn the silly season into the sanity season. They aim to bring us closer to the one we love.

96 pages, ISBN 978-2-89688-966-6

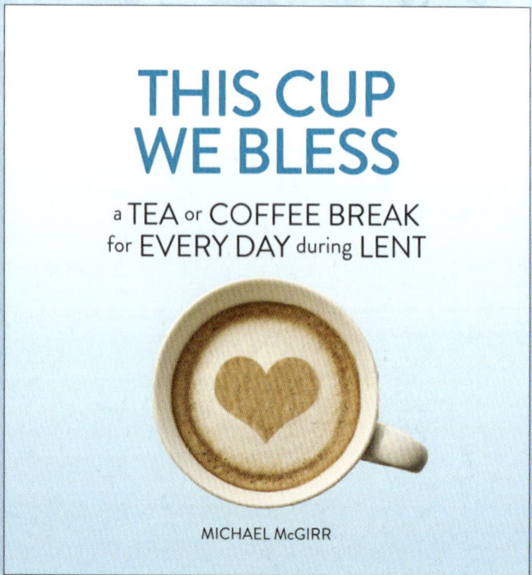

This book is an invitation to drink deep, to find God in the ordinary moments of every day during Lent. It is about the cup you share in the lunchroom with a colleague to get through the day. It is about the cup someone puts beside your keyboard as you work late into the night. It is about the cup a friend holds to your lips when you can't manage it for yourself. These are the cups which, in the words of Scripture, are really brimming over.

On the night before he died, Jesus begged, 'Father, if you are willing, remove this cup from me; yet, not my will but yours be done.' As we travel through Lent, we also accept whatever cup comes our way. This book will help us all on our journey to new life.

96 pages, ISBN 978-2-89830-097-4

Available in Canada from Novalis: en.novalis.ca or 1-800-387-7164 (toll-free)

Available in the United States from Twenty-Third Publications: twentythirdpublications.com